In Memory of

Roger E. Allen

Presented by His Loving
Wife & Children

Mary Allen

Brad Allen

Nancy Talarico

Betsy Jones

2005

# Richard Wagner
## and German Opera

# Richard Wagner
## and German Opera

Donna Getzinger
Daniel Felsenfeld

# MORGAN
# REYNOLDS
### Publishing, Inc.

620 South Elm Street, Suite 223
Greensboro, North Carolina  27406
http://www.morganreynolds.com

# Classical Composers

Johann Sebastian Bach

Antonio Vivaldi

Richard Wagner

Johannes Brahms

George Frideric Handel

# RICHARD WAGNER AND GERMAN OPERA

Library of Congress Cataloging-in-Publication Data

Getzinger, Donna.
    Richard Wagner and German opera / Donna Getzinger and Daniel Felsenfeld.
        v. cm. — (Classical composers)
        Includes bibliographical references (p.   ) and index.
        Contents: Growing Up in the Theater — Conducting and Composing — Paris — Success and Revolution — From Exile to the *Ring* — Music and the Muse — Homeless in the Homeland — The King — A Theater of His Own — The Legacy — Timeline.
        ISBN 1-931798-24-9 (library binding)
        1. Wagner, Richard, 1813-1883—Juvenile literature. 2. Composers—Germany—Biography—Juvenile literature. [1. Wagner, Richard, 1813-1883. 2. Composers.] I. Felsenfeld, Daniel. II. Title. III. Series.
        ML3930.W2G38 2004
        782.1'092—dc22

                        2003026728

Printed in the United States of America
First Edition

*To Lucy and Maggie Machlahn*

# Contents

Richard Wagner (1813-1883)
*(Photograph by F. Hanfstaengl, Munich.)*

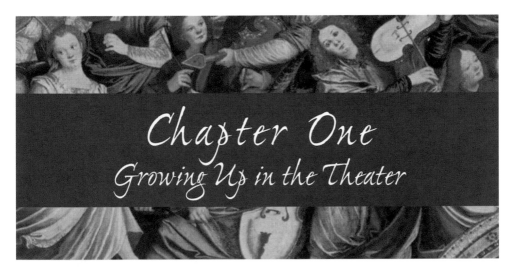

# Chapter One
## Growing Up in the Theater

After one of Richard Wagner's many fights with his second wife, Cosima, she wrote in her diary that, during their reconciliation, he had taken her in his arms "and said that we loved each other too passionately; that was the cause of our sufferings." This intimate moment from Wagner's chaotic personal life reveals much about the character and artistic vision of one of the nineteenth century's most important composers.

Wagner was a passionate man, and this might have been necessary for him to write his operatic masterpieces. His belief that desire caused great suffering proved true as he became involved in multiple adulterous love affairs, sometimes with the wives of his friends. His nature also led him to spend money he did not have on fine clothes and extravagant furnishings, and then to flee from his unpaid creditors.

This same passion also drove him to embrace dangerous ideas and theories, such as his belief in German superiority and his advocacy of anti-Semitic views. One of the greatest composers in history, Wagner will always be inextricably linked to Adolf Hitler, whose racial and nationalistic ideas led to the the twentieth century's most destructive war. Richard Wagner is one of the most complicated and controversial composers in the history of western music.

Wagner's life was lived in almost constant chaos, so it seems fitting that he was born in the middle of both political and personal turbulence. The political turbulence, which had turned into military conflict by 1813, the year of Wagner's birth, grew out of the French Revolution. Beginning in 1789, the French populace rose in revolt against the old monarchial order. By 1793 the king and his immediate

The French Revolution ushered in dramatic changes to the country's social and political structures, as feudalism was done away with and the middle class began to rise. *(Courtesy of the Library of Congress.)*

family had met their deaths on the newly invented guillotine. By the end of the decade the revolution had been hijacked by the gifted Corsican military officer Napoleon Bonaparte, who crowned himself emperor and then began a fifteen year campaign to conquer Europe.

The Napoleonic Wars reached their zenith in the years 1813 to 1815. Over the course of these two years a series of battles and naval conflicts eventually led to Napoleon's defeat and exile. One of the most decisive battles of this last phase of the Napoleonic Wars took place at Leipzig, a town in the eastern German territory of Saxony. The French army was largely outnumbered at this point, but their offer of peace was refused. The allies attacked the town, where the French were holed up, and more than a hundred thousand soldiers were killed in a bloody three-day campaign.

Richard Wagner was born in Leipzig on May 22, 1813. As the battle raged around them, Wagner's mother prayed her son would grow up to live in more peaceful times. But Wagner's fate was sealed—he would always live in tumult.

This grand political and military conflict, the dissonant clash of battle, the patriotic call to arms against the hated French invaders, and the exaltation of myth and intense emotion pervaded the impressionable Wagner's early years. But this external conflict was only part of the story. An even more powerful drama played out at the very core of young Wagner's family life.

Richard was the last of nine children born to Friedrich and Johanna Wagner, though there is good reason to doubt that Friedrich was actually Richard's biological father.

The house in which Richard Wagner was born, in Leipzig.

Friedrich died of typhoid a few months after Richard was born. Nine months later, Johanna married Ludwig Geyer, a family friend, and six months later she gave birth to a daughter, Cäcilie. Ludwig Geyer was likely Richard's father, too. They bore a striking physical resemblance. For most of his childhood, the person we know as Richard Wagner went by the name of Richard Geyer. He would not return to his baptismal name until he was a teenager and Ludwig Geyer had passed away.

Geyer was an actor in the Dresden Court Theater. He also painted and sang in some of the musical productions. Wagner grew up in the middle of the capital city of Saxony, immersed in the ceaseless drama of the theater. Nearly all of Wagner's siblings would choose some type of theatrical career. Richard spent his early years backstage, surrounded by the costumes, scenery, actors, and music of the theater. He even went onstage in some small roles as a child.

Richard was close to Ludwig Geyer, who loved him deeply in return and saw to it that the boy he believed to be his son had a good education. He was the first to introduce Richard to music and to the piano. Geyer eventually developed tuberculosis, a lung disease that was almost always fatal at the time, and he grew progressively weaker. When Richard was eight, he was brought home from boarding school to say good-bye. He played a tune for his dying father that convinced Ludwig his son had musical talent, though Ludwig died only a few days later and would never see that talent come to fruition.

After Geyer's death, the family moved several times. Though they had little money, all of the children except Richard received some kind of musical training. Johanna

Ludwig Geyer, the man who raised Richard and was probably his biological father.

Richard's mother, Johanna Wagner. *(Courtesy of Wagner-Gedenkstäte, Beyreuth.)*

wanted at least one of her children to pursue a more legitimate career than the theater, and she chose Richard to be the one. Despite not having lessons, young Richard was drawn to the piano and captivated by music. Rosalie, his oldest sister, worked as an actress at the Dresden Court Theater. When Johanna and the younger children lived with Rosalie for a time, Richard was again back in the world of imagination that he loved.

The Dresden Court Theater presented stage plays, operas, and light musicals. Theater was very popular in the early nineteenth century. There was a growing middle class that had money to spend on entertainment, and theaters of all types were popular places to be entertained. While theater had its roots in ancient Greece, opera was a relatively new form—the first modern opera was Claudio Monteverdi's *Orfeo,* which was performed in 1607. Operas are essentially plays that are sung instead of spoken. In the two centuries of opera's existence it was enhanced with lavish costumes and dazzling scenery. It was a grand visual pageant as well as a musical style.

Opera had been born in Italy, and for decades Italian opera was considered to be the best. The German composer and impresario George Frideric Handel took Italian opera to London and died a wealthy man. Gradually, other nationalities adapted the operatic form to their own

Claudio Monteverdi is considered the father of opera. His *Orfeo* is the first successful example of the art form. *(Courtesy of Tiroler Museum, Ferdinandeum, Innsbruck.)*

languages, myths, and customs. In the late eighteenth century, the Austrian composer Wolfgang Amadeus Mozart took German opera to new, magnificent heights. German composer Carl Maria von Weber, an old friend of Ludwig Geyer's, wrote the opera *Der Freischultz (The Marksman)* using German folklore as his subject, and its music was popular in the Geyer household and throughout the land.

By Wagner's time there was a large, enthusiastic German audience for opera. Composers wrote music and librettists wrote the books, or lyrics, as quickly as possible, and rushed them to the stage. Audiences clamored for more, and loved to hear their favorite arias (extended solos that give singers the chance to show off their vocal prowess), sung by their

Wolfgang Amadeus Mozart. *(Courtesy of Internationale Stiftung Mozarteum, Salzburg.)*

favorite singers, again and again.

Richard fell in love with opera at an early age, but his mother stubbornly resisted her son's attraction to the arts. She insisted he go to school and pursue a more stable career. When a poem he wrote for school was published, she hoped he might become a writer. Richard did like to write, but he hated school and was a poor student. When his mother went with Rosalie to Prague and left him behind, Richard promptly dropped out of school and spent his days roaming the city and writing a dramatic piece he was sure would be his masterwork. He was thirteen years old.

Another of Richard's sisters, Luisa, had moved back to Leipzig to work at the Leipzig theater. Since he was mostly unsupervised, Richard was free to visit her there. In Leipzig he made the acquaintance of his uncle, Adolf Wagner, whom he admired. His new relationship with, and respect for, Adolf Wagner was part of the reason he gave up the name Geyer and reverted back to his birth name, Wagner. His other reason was not nearly as innocent.

While there is no evidence Ludwig Geyer had Jewish ancestry, the name Geyer was sometimes associated with Jews. Many in Leipzig even assumed he was at least partly

Jewish. Apparently, young Richard did not want the same assumption to be made about him.

Wagner seems to have adopted hatred for the Jewish people at an early age. Called anti-Semitism, this hatred had been an unfortunate element of European culture for centuries. During the plague (the Black Death) of the late fifteenth century, for example, Jews all over the continent were attacked and killed due to rumors they had poisoned wells or were themselves the cause of the plague. Jews were also often barred from entering into certain professions or learning specific skills. As well, rulers would sometimes divert attention from their own failures and corruption by shifting focus to certain groups, including the Jews.

There had been improvements over the centuries though, and by the early nineteenth century it seemed to many Jews that they might finally become part of mainstream culture in some European nations. Germany, in particular, became a place where large numbers of Jewish people prospered. Often, German Jews felt pressured to assimilate into the majority culture, and many even converted to Christianity. Some became leading nationalists and, in the face of the French conquest under Napoleon Bonaparte, supported the idea of a unified German state.

This German pride and nationalist sentiment would eventually unify the dozens of independent states, principalities, and free cities into one nation, and give rise to a new, ultimately more destructive form of anti-Semitism. As German nationalist intellectuals, students, and other patriots began organizing and writing, there also began a process of defining exactly what qualities made up a true German. This intellectual ferment went in several directions, of course, but a segment of the nationalists determined that Jews would always be more loyal to members of their own religion than to a German state; that it was therefore impossible to be both Jewish and a loyal German.

Perhaps inevitably, racial theories designed to support these ideas began circulating. Over the next decades some of the new, startling scientific ideas such as Charles Darwin's theory of natural selection, and radical political ideas such as anarchism and communism, were sometimes incorporated into anti-Semitism. To some, this gave anti-Semitism a firmer intellectual and moral foundation.

Another critical force in the development of political anti-Semitism was the rise of the industrial, urban economy. More and more, people became dependent on forces beyond their control for their livelihood. Large sections of the population were subjected to economic depressions and other rapid shifts in the economy. In the crowded, dirty cities jobs were lost, gained, and lost again at a dizzying rate for people who, a generation before, had lived in small agricultural villages and on farms; entire professions were replaced by new technologies in short periods. Governments were not always responsive to these changes and people were enveloped by fear and uncertainty. In their anger, many people adopted a new version of political anti-Semitism that would grow and finally erupt in the savagery of the early twentieth century.

It is impossible, of course, to know precisely why Wagner

adopted anti-Semitism as an integral part of his worldview. The reason probably lies in a combination of psychological, political, and intellectual factors. What is known is that even at an early age, and despite the fact he loved his father very much, he rejected the name Geyer to erase any suggestion that he might come from Jewish roots. This prejudice would continue to grow throughout his life.

While in Leipzig, Richard met several young men who were students at Leipzig University. He was enraptured by everything about them. He wanted nothing more than to wear a fraternity jacket, sit around in cafes all day, and discuss art and revolution. He returned to Dresden to pack the rest of his things and move to Leipzig.

Johanna Geyer and her daughters had also returned to Leipzig and young Richard appeared on their doorstep. His mother was upset that he had dropped out of school, and made him promise to enroll in the St. Nicholas School in Leipzig. He did, but did so poorly on the entrance exams that they put him back a grade. Richard was furious and insulted, and began to skip classes as often as he could think of reasons not to go.

Richard spent as much time as he could with his Uncle Adolf. He worshipped the older man, and wrote plays in an effort to please him. Adolf was amused by his nephew's efforts and, despite his reservations about encouraging Richard's delinquency, he shared his own love of literature and music with the boy. For the first time, Richard heard music composed by the great Ludwig van Beethoven. He was shattered to learn the German composer had died only

The city of Leipzig, Richard Wagner's birthplace and home for many years. Regarded as a major center of commerce and education, Leipzig boasted one of the most progressive universities in Germany. *(Courtesy of Museum für Geschichte der Stadt, Leipzig.)*

a few years before, in 1827. Carl Maria von Weber also died while Richard was in Leipzig, in 1826. Weber's were the first examples of German Romantic opera, and his combining German folklore and nationalism impacted Wagner's own later compositions. Learning of the two composers' deaths hit the boy hard. He felt abandoned by the men whose music he craved to know more about, as though their deaths were a personal insult. He felt that Germany had been abandoned as well, and soon decided that he was the only one who could fill the musical void. Richard Wagner would be the next great voice of German music.

For a young man with almost no musical experience, this was quite a goal. But Richard had made up his mind, and he systematically prepared to write his first opera by setting a play he had written to music. He checked out a book on how to write music from a library. He kept the book for so long that he ran up tremendous fines he could not afford to pay and had to be bailed out by his mother. This was the first of many, many debts to come.

Young Wagner skipped almost six months of school to devote himself to writing his opera *Leubald*. When it was finally finished, he sent the manuscript to his uncle, along with a note suggesting Adolf could explain to Johanna why school was no longer necessary for her son, the musical genius. Adolf informed his sister-in-law of the boy's activities and the whole family was called in for a conference. Adolf had to confess that *Leubald* was not the work of a prodigy. It might be prudent to consider alternate careers, just in case Richard was not the musical genius he believed himself to be. In the end, Richard was bribed with an offer of music lessons to return to school.

This first opera contains the seeds of Wagner's later work. *Leubald* borrows generously from the dramatic stories Richard had been exposed to, but the plot forecasts much of what was to come later. However, the score for *Leubald* proves that he badly needed the music lessons the writing of the opera indirectly earned him. But the lessons were not a great success. Richard proved to be a desultory violinist who mostly refused to practice and tortured his family's ears when he did. And despite promises to his mother, he continued to skip school.

One of the few things that Richard wanted to do was study composition. He was fortunate to have a family in the arts. His brother-in-law, Heinrich Wolfram, understood the young man's desire and helped him to get access to some of Beethoven's scores. Richard threw himself into the study of those precious pages, and showed an uncanny aptitude for understanding the nuance and complexity of composition. He copied the score of Beethoven's Ninth Symphony, and then rewrote it as a piece for piano—a remarkable achievement only possible because of Wagner's inherent talent.

Beethoven's Ninth Symphony captivated and, briefly, obsessed Wagner. He was drawn to the piece because it embodied the same Romantic qualities found in the works of his favorite author, E. T. A. Hoffmann. The artists of the Romantic age valued emotion over reason. Beethoven's Ninth Symphony, a sprawling, dramatic piece rumored to have been written as the composer was driven nearly mad by his deafness, made it the definitive masterwork of Romantic music. Many thought it a more authentic work of art than the comparatively restrained, intellectual music of the earlier Classical and Baroque eras. Writers in the Romantic tradition, like Hoffmann (who was also a composer), wrote gothic tales designed to elicit strong emotions from their readers. Hoffmann took much of his inspiration for his stories from myths and folktales. A hugely popular writer, his works have been imitated and reworked endlessly, and inspired the classic ballet, *The Nut-cracker.*

German Romanticism differed from the artistic movement in other countries, mainly because it was so closely tied to the idea of German nationalism. The tendency among Germans was to embrace their own heritage, folklore, and history, even if it meant dis-

The great German composer Ludwig van Beethoven. *(Archiv für Kunst und Geschichte, Berlin.)*

criminating against other cultures. Wagner was not the only convert to the nationalist cause.

Though Richard was not a strong student, he still wanted to go to university. He changed schools again, determined to find one that would recommend his admittance to higher education when he was old enough. In the meantime, he filled his days seeing as many concerts and operas as he could. Once more, his family connections proved valuable. His eldest sister, Rosalie, came to Leipzig in a touring company and Richard had access to free tickets.

The company performed Beethoven's opera *Fidelio*. The female lead was an opera singer of great fame, Wilhelmine Schröder-Devrient. Though she was only twenty-four,

Schröder-Devrient was already a huge star. Her voice was strong, but it was her acting ability and attractive figure that made her exceptional. Richard Wagner was stunned by her performance, and immediately returned home to compose a letter to her. In his autobiography, he remembered writing: "if in the days to come she should ever hear my name praised in the world of Art, she must remember that she had that evening made me what I then swore it was my destiny to become."

The first satisfying piece of music Richard wrote was his Overture in B-flat. The conductor at the Leipzig theater was a friend of Rosalie's and a champion of new artists. He agreed to perform it at a free Christmas Eve concert for poor residents of the city. Seventeen-year-old Wagner was thrilled.

The overture was highly influenced by Beethoven, and Wagner wanted to communicate though his music the mystical feelings and messages he heard in Beethoven's. He even wrote the musicians' parts in different colored inks in order to better indicate the feelings he wanted portrayed. After each color played, the change in emotion was signaled by a stroke on the timpani drum. This first, grand experiment did not work. As the single stroke was repeated over and over again between passages, the audience went from disbelieving silence to muffled snickering to laughing out loud. Humiliated, Wagner ran from the theater.

After this ignominious debut, Wagner put aside his compositions for a time and concentrated on getting into college. Unfortunately, his poor grades and spotty attendance made acceptance unlikely. He was undaunted by these challenges—he simply went to the rector of the university and asked to be admitted as a part-time student. The rector was willing to accommodate the bold young man, and by spring, Richard Wagner was a university student, and a fraternity member, just as he had planned.

# Chapter Two
## Conducting and Composing

The University of Leipzig turned out not to be everything Wagner had hoped. The first problem was that he was expected to attend classes and the second was that most of the young men at the school were wealthy—none of them wore old-fashioned clothes or had families who made their livings in the theater. Wagner was acutely sensitive to his relative poverty and began borrowing money to keep up false appearances.

His mostly unsupervised childhood had given Wagner a sense of independence that often made him difficult to get along with. He had a fierce temper and was constantly challenging fellow students to duels. A small, fragile man with little experience fighting, it was through luck alone that his challenges were dismissed or avoided. This good luck, however, did little to help him learn to control his emotions.

The organist and director of the St. Thomas Church, Christian Theodor Weinlig, also taught composition at the university. He found teaching Wagner to be a challenge. After several frustrating, fruitless lessons, Weinlig threatened to have Wagner expelled if he did not buckle down and concentrate. In his typically rebellious fashion, Wagner then defied his teacher's expectations and became his best student.

At first delighted by this turn around, Weinlig was soon overwhelmed by the amount of information his student could absorb. They began with the music of Johann Sebastian Bach. Wagner studied his scores with an intensity that amazed his instructor. In eight weeks, he had mastered the complicated musical forms of fugue and counterpoint—the essential components of Bach's work. Weinlig next turned to the works of Mozart and Beethoven, only to find Wagner already knew

Johann Sebastian Bach's complicated compositions were readily absorbed by young Wagner.
*(Courtesy of Museum für Geschichte der Stadt, Leipzig.)*

Beethoven as well as he did. Mozart was a revelation to the young man. Weinlig also arranged for the publication of some early sonatas Wagner wrote during this time. After only six months of study, Weinlig dismissed his student, saying that he had not only mastered

Wagner's first music teacher, Christian Theodor Weinlig.

all of the musical techniques, but had achieved "independence" and did not need more lessons.

Fraternity life turned out to be a disappointment and, after Weinlig dismissed him, Wagner left the university. However, with Weinlig's encouragement, he continued to compose. His early works were immature, but showed promise. His sister Rosalie again intervened to have her brother's work performed, though the timpani incident had not been forgotten. This time, Wagner's name was not announced or printed on the program until it was clear that audiences enjoyed his music. They did, and Wagner was on his way to respectability.

In spring of 1832, Wagner turned nineteen. He was old enough now to pay some attention to the world outside of his own existence, and what he found there moved him deeply. When the Confederation of German States was formed in 1815, the territory that is now Poland was split

This map of the Hapsburg Empire, c. 1765, shows many areas crucial to the development of western music—Vienna, Venice, Dresden, and Leipzig among them. At the same time as powerful music and art were rising out of these cultural centers, political structures and even national boundaries were undergoing tumultuous periods of shifting and redefinition. In the 1800s, nationalism was on the rise throughout Europe, and by the early twentieth century, the political landscape would again be disrupted as the first World War broke out.

Frédéric Chopin, in an 1849 photograph.
*(Courtesy of The Royal College of Music, London.)*

between Austria and Russia. During the early 1830s, Polish patriots rose up against the repressive Tsar Nicholas I of Russia. The Poles fought fiercely but were no match for the Russian army. Twenty-five thousand Poles were killed in battle and the rest were sent, along with their families, to the frozen tundra of Siberia. Some fled westward to avoid such a fate. Thousands of Poles came through Leipzig on their way to safe haven in France. One of the refugees was Frédéric Chopin, the virtuoso pianist and composer. Seeing the plight of the Poles made Wagner sympathetic to patriot causes, and reinforced his nationalist tendencies.

After his early musical successes, Wagner decided to write a novel in the style of E.T.A. Hoffmann. He did not get very far before realizing he could combine his musical talent with his love of literature by writing an opera. *Die Hochzeit (The Wedding),* another of his early attempts at opera, was a dark and tragic story about a bride who kills her lover.

Wagner wrote in secret, hurrying to hide his manuscript

if footsteps neared his door. Once the libretto, or story, was finished, Wagner showed it to only one person—his sister Rosalie. Her opinion was the only one that mattered to him. She was one of the two members of the family who had not yet written him off as a wastrel. His other supporter was their mother; over the years it was Rosalie who convinced the older woman not to give up on her son. Rosalie was also the breadwinner of the family who took in and supported her younger siblings and surviving parent. No copy of *Die Hochzeit* survives, as Wagner promptly destroyed the pa-

Wagner's sister Rosalie. One of his most valued critics, she greatly influenced many of his early musical choices.

pers when Rosalie expressed reservations about the story. Wagner would never show a work in progress to anyone again.

His next piece, a symphony in C Major, had a better reception. In January of 1833, it was performed at the Leipzig Schneider-Herbage, one of the best concert halls in the city. Critics and audiences enjoyed the piece, and Wagner's family was pleased he seemed to be finally making something of himself. Rosalie introduced her brother to a well-known local author, Heinrich Laube, who served as the music critic for a local paper and had praised Wagner's work. Later, Laube approached Wagner about composing the score to an opera libretto he had written. Wagner was flattered by the offer, which could have meant quick fame and fortune, but said he wanted to write both the words and the music. Laube was surprised by Wagner's rebuff, but took it gracefully, and the two became good friends.

Wagner did indeed plan to write both the words and the music for his own operas, and had been working on a new libretto ever since he tore up the one Rosalie rejected. His new piece was called *Die Feen (The Fairies)* and was based on a tale written by Carlo Gozzi in the eighteenth century. It is a magical story about a man who falls in love with a mysterious woman who is half-fairy and half-human. She goes through a series of trials in an effort to become fully human, but in the end becomes an immortal fairy. Throughout his career, Wagner would be drawn to mythology and fairy tales for the basis of his stories.

Encouraged by the success of his symphony, and by

Laube's admiration, Wagner set out to find a proper musical post. His family was there to help. His older brother Albert was a singer and stage manager at a theater in the nearby town of Würzburg. Albert used his influence to find his little brother a position as choirmaster. In January of 1833, nineteen-year-old Richard caught a ride in a farmer's cart.

The job of choirmaster paid very little but was a great training ground. Operas generally use soloists in leading roles, but there is often a chorus as well. Wagner's job at Würzburg was to direct the chorus, which included teaching them their parts. At first, he felt he was in over his head, as the work was totally new to him. But in his typical fashion, he plunged ahead and was soon able to enjoy his position. He also gained a good amount of useful experience and knowledge from the time he spent working with the cast backstage. It helped him to understand what could and could not be done in a production, and how to best handle all the intricate and complicated details of an opera.

Working in a theater energized Wagner, and he spent all of his free time over the course of the next year composing the score to *Die Feen*. While the music of this early opera lacks the depth and originality that would come in his later works, it does offer some insight into the development of Wagnerian techniques. *Die Feen* is the first opera to use what would become a Wagner trademark: *leitmotifs*. A leitmotif is a short melody that represents a character, feeling, object, or idea. By repeating the melody each time that character, feeling, object, or idea is referred to, the composer can more closely connect the music to the action.

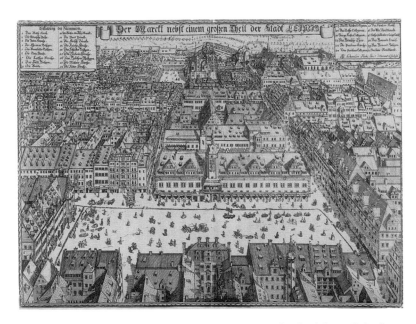

Leipzig, as portrayed in an eighteenth-century engraving by Johann Schreiber.

Leitmotifs also serve as clues to the audience and help them to interpret or understand the unfolding drama. Wagner's use of leitmotifs was an innovation that changed the way operas were both written and understood.

His first season at the Würzburg Theater ended with the arrival of fall. To earn money while he finished his opera, Wagner found work conducting concerts with the Würzburg Musical Society. Through the society, he heard his symphony, overtures, and parts of *Die Feen* performed. Bolstered by his success in Würzburg, Wagner returned to Leipzig after Christmas with the finished score of his first opera. He hoped to have it performed in its entirety. Rosalie professed to like this new piece, and she personally approached Leipzig's theater director about staging it. The director waffled on his decision for months, first saying he would do it, then finding all sorts of reasons to postpone the production. But after more than six months had passed, it was clear *Die Feen* would not be performed in Leipzig.

What Wagner perceived as Leipzig's rejection of his music hurt him deeply. He thought that his hometown would be more supportive, especially since he was writing in the style of the great German composers like Weber, which was the kind of music they enjoyed. In his frustration, he responded by turning against the German music he so loved. For Wagner, Italian opera suddenly came to represent the light, sophisticated work of a happier and more refined people. He wrote an article lauding the music of the Italian composers Vincenzo Bellini and Gioaccinno Rossini. A performance by his favorite singer, Wilhelmine Schröder-Devrient, in a Bellini opera confirmed what he called the "inconceivable charm" of Italian music. To prove his devotion to this style, he began writing a new opera in a distinctly comedic Italian form called *opera buffa*. He called this opera *Das Liebesverbot (The Love Ban)* and based its plot loosely on William Shakespeare's play *Measure for Measure*.

Meanwhile, the Leipzig Theater director had been besieged by Wagner for nearly a year and was only able to untangle himself from the passionate young man by finding him a job elsewhere. The Magdeburg Theater Company needed a conductor, and he sent Wagner there to apply. The company was a touring troupe, run by an unpredictable man named Heinrich Bethmann. When Wagner arrived, he was shocked to discover the troupe was in total disarray. A performance was scheduled for a few days later, but the musicians were refusing to rehearse. Bethmann met Wagner at the door wearing only a dressing gown, and his wife openly flaunted her lover. Wagner resolved not to take the job. He went to find rooms for the night so he could return to Leipzig first thing in the morning.

That night, Wagner stayed in a boarding house. While there, he met a beautiful young woman who happened to live in the room above. Her name was Minna Planer, and she was the lead actress in the Magdeburg Company. Instantly smitten, Wagner decided to accept the conductor's job. But his primary goal was to win Minna's love.

Minna Planer acted because she was good at it, not because she loved it. Her real desire was to marry well and to maintain a home and raise children. Her beauty had

The Magdeburg Theater. Wagner's employment there was full of tumult.

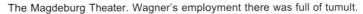

Minna Planer, Wagner's first wife. *(The Burrell Collection, Curtis Institute of Music, Philadelphia.)*

captivated many actors and musicians, but she usually resisted their advances. She did not want to live a life in the theater or marry a starving actor or artist. Richard Wagner was several years her junior, and a penniless conductor at the very beginning of his career, which was exactly the type she was trying to avoid. Yet she found him attractive; his self-confidence charmed her. While she made sure the landlady of the boarding house locked her door every night, as a precaution against his obvious passions, she also encouraged Wagner's affections. Years later, Wagner would recall the beginning of their relationship: "My association with my kindly housemate soon became a passionate addiction, and she returned the ingeniously impetuous advances of the twenty-one-year-old conductor with a certain tolerant amazement."

Their budding affair was one bright spot in an otherwise difficult situation in Magdeburg. Wagner conducted his first opera within a week of being hired. While the experience was very good for his education, none of the operas in the company's repertoire were to his taste. They were all light and fluffy works that he found quite dull. Bethmann was a poor businessman, and salaries were rarely paid on time—if at all. For several months, Wagner and the company toured the backwaters of small German towns, until they finally returned to Magdeburg for a much-needed rest.

The Magdeburg Theater Company played a half-year season in its hometown, and the theatergoers there made Wagner's job more palatable. Conducting before friendly and appreciative crowds, Wagner grew more popular with each performance, and the recognition he received pleased him. Soon it seemed everyone knew the young conductor, and Wagner came to consider himself one of the "bigwigs of opera," if only in a small town.

In Wagner's time, operas and plays were usually put on in the same theater. One night audiences might see Shakespeare's *Macbeth,* the next Mozart's opera *The Magic Flute.* Theaters were built for entertainment, but they were also social centers. Their design encouraged audiences to talk and move around during performances. The seats were divided to the right and the left by a center aisle, and faced each other rather than the stage. The lights stayed brightly lit while the performance went on, so audiences could read their programs (and the translations of operas that were performed in foreign languages), or watch one another. The actors had the audience's full attention only when a soloist was performing an aria. Of all the performers, the conductor was most visible, because he stood on a platform in full view of the audience.

Being a conductor suited Wagner. He enjoyed the applause and the recognition and quickly assumed a lifestyle that befit his popularity. He gave parties and bought expensive furniture and fine clothes. But the Magdeburg Company did not pay well, and he went into debt almost immediately. His debts caused problems with Minna—creditors were constantly at the door of the boardinghouse, and when Wagner refused to see them, they often harassed Minna for payment. She was not impressed by his inability to control his spending, and she ended their relationship. Wagner was devastated.

Determined to pay off his creditors and win Minna back, Wagner came up with a plan. He would conduct a special benefit concert—for himself. In order to assure a

A young opera singer. Great soloists commanded the audience's attention and were treated like stars by their admiring fans. (*Courtesy of Civico Museo Bibliografico Musicale, Bologna.*)

large crowd, he asked the great soprano Schröder-Devrient to appear. She had heard his music and seen him conduct; believing him to be an artist with great potential, she agreed. Wagner put up posters and advertisements all over the city, with Schröder-Devrient's name in bold letters. He was positive the concert would improve his fortune, and he rashly told all his creditors to come to his door the morning after to receive their money.

The concert was a disaster. No one believed the young conductor had really convinced the great star to sing, so hardly anyone bought tickets. Wagner was horrified to see Schröder-Devrient singing to a nearly empty house. The next morning, his creditors appeared and Wagner was ashamed to admit he could not pay them. His pockets were as empty as they had ever been.

As soon as he was able to, Wagner returned to Leipzig. He was broke, deeply in debt, and Minna refused even to speak to him. He did not want to sign on for another season at Magdeburg because the pay was so low. He worked to complete *Das Liebesverbot* and sought out opportunities to have his music played or his operas produced. To his sorrow, not a single theater in Leipzig showed any interest in his work. Instead, everyone was clamoring for the composer Felix Mendelssohn. Mendelssohn's music recalled the Baroque and Classical eras and sounded old-fashioned to Wagner, but audiences loved it. Once again, Wagner could not find the support he needed in his hometown.

When the king of Prussia offered to put money into the nearly bankrupt Magdeburg Theater Company, Wagner changed his mind about returning. He missed Minna very much, and his prospects in Leipzig had not panned out. He negotiated a new, higher-paying contract, and looked forward to putting on operas that were more to his taste.

The new season in Magdeburg did not turn out the way Wagner imagined. He arrived in town only to find that Minna was on her way out. She had taken a job with a theater in Berlin. Wagner could not stand to lose her twice and rashly proposed marriage. Minna was shocked but she accepted his proposal and returned to Magdeburg as his fiancée.

In the spring of 1836, the Magdeburg Theater Company staged the first—and only—performance of *Das Liebesverbot*. It was another disaster. The actors were tired from a long season and refused to rehearse the new show unless they were paid extra. Their demands were not met, so the curtain opened on a cast who had to be fed their lines by the conductor. There was supposed to be a second performance, but a fistfight between the lead actress's lover and her husband forced a cancellation. Wagner was counting on the revenue from the performance to pay off his debts. When that money did not appear, he fled town to avoid being put in debtor's prison.

The Königsberg Theater in Prussia came to the rescue by offering Minna a contract. She accepted, and promised to try to find a position for Wagner. The theater already had a musical director, but the manager told Minna he preferred Wagner's work. He also told her of a theater being constructed in Riga, a city in Russia. As soon as it was ready, he wanted Wagner to go there with him to run the company.

The earliest known portrait of Richard Wagner.

Minna sent for her fiancé and the Königsberg Theater gave him a small retainer to keep him in town until either the current musical director left or the Riga Theater was completed.

Their time in Königsberg should have been happy, but it was there Wagner discovered that Minna had taken another lover during their time apart. He was insane with jealousy, but Minna kept her cool. Their engagement had seemed hasty and she was not convinced Wagner really intended to marry her. Her infidelity made up his mind— he wanted to get married as soon as possible. The young couple fought constantly, and years later Wagner would tell the story of a terrible argument they had on the doorstep of the man who was to marry them: "Not a little embarrassed at having surprised us in the act of quarreling, [the parson] invited us in. We were obliged to put a good face on the matter, however, and the absurdity of the situation so tickled our sense of humor that we laughed; the parson was appeased, and the wedding fixed for eleven o'clock the next morning." Minna and Richard Wagner were married on November 24, 1836. He was twenty-three years old.

Five months later, Wagner became musical director at the Königsberg Theater. Two months later, the theater went bankrupt and Wagner was again out of a job. Tension in the Wagner household ran high. The couple's livelihood was uncertain, yet Wagner continued to spend recklessly. Six months after their wedding, Wagner came home from a rehearsal to find that Minna had run off to Dresden with a wealthy playboy. Wagner spent the summer chasing her from town to town, trying to convince her to come back to him, though he knew he was unable to provide the kind of stable life she craved. Finally, in August of 1837, the Riga Theater opened.

Life in Russia was an adjustment for Wagner. He was still resentful about the Russian treatment of the Poles five years before, and it rankled him to see Russian officials strolling the streets. He also had to accept the fact that Riga wanted only light Italian opera, not the music he preferred. Finally, the news came that his sister Rosalie had died. He had not seen her in two years, and her death struck him deeply. The one bright spot in his life was Minna's return. Soon after he arrived in Riga, she showed up at his door, contrite and hoping for reconciliation. He took her back.

The next project to capture Wagner's imagination was inspired by a novel called *Rienzi, the Last of the Tribunes*. It is about a man, Rienzi, who fights the nobility of his city for the freedom of its people. Rienzi has the support of the populace, but in the end the nobles are too clever and treacherous, and he is killed. Wagner envisioned the story as a five-act grand opera, the kind of sophisticated work that his sister Rosalie would have admired. He wrote the libretto quickly and then began work on the score.

Until this point, Wagner had written his operas and musical pieces for practical reasons—he wanted to have them performed in order to make money. He was used to second-rate theaters and often had to accept changes because of inferior performers or tight budgets. But now he set his mind on debuting *Rienzi* in Paris, in a magnificent opera house with a first-rate cast, and he began writing an opera worthy of such an event.

Riga seemed smaller and smaller to Wagner, and he would never be happy there. Minna supported her husband's plan to premiere his opera in Paris. They decided that after their second season in Riga, in the summer of 1839, they would make their way to Paris, the city of their dreams.

# Chapter Three
## Paris

Dreaming of going to Paris was one thing, accomplishing it was another. Leaving Riga was not easy; the couple had little money and creditors hounded them. Wagner was so deeply in debt he was not granted a passport for fear he would skip out on his debts. The couple decided to sell as many of their possessions as they could, and Wagner conducted another benefit concert for himself. They were only able to generate enough money to pay off a few old debts, and were still far from clearing up the newer ones.

In desperation, Wagner decided he had little choice but to sneak over the border. A friend helped to arrange their passage, and in June of 1839, the couple packed their belongings into a carriage and set off on a two-day trip to the border, where they camped in a smuggler's den until it was safely dark. Russian guards patrolled, and the Wagners had only a few minutes while the guards changed shifts to run across a ravine to the coach waiting for them on the Prussian side. If they were spotted, they would be shot dead. Luck was on their side that night, and they crossed un-harmed.

Once in Prussia, they took a rickety carriage to the coast. On the way, the carriage overturned and Minna was badly injured—she had been pregnant and the accident caused a miscarriage. After they made it to the coast, Minna was able to rest for a few days until Richard found the captain of a ship headed to England who was willing to take the fugitives aboard. They had to sneak onto the ship from a dinghy, and hide from the customs inspectors among the cargo.

On their ocean voyage, they encountered heavy winds and violent weather that blew the ship off course. The journey ended up taking three and half weeks, instead of the expected eight days, to complete. At times, the Wagners feared for their lives. Safely in London, they comforted themselves by seeing the sights and enjoying the restau-rants, which further depleted their already low reserves of money. Getting to France required another boat ride, but this one proved to be more fortuitous. On board, Wagner made the acquaintance of two women who were friends of the composer Giacomo Meyerbeer. Even luckier, Meyerbeer was living in Boulogne, where the ship would dock, and the ladies offered to arrange an introduction.

Giacomo Meyerbeer was a famous and popular com-poser. Originally from Prussia, he was also Jewish. Having earlier studied with Weber, he now wrote grand operas that were all the rage in Paris. History has come to find most of his music shallow, but he was a hero of his time. His music was highly influential. Wagner was honored to have an introduction and decided to stay in Boulogne for a few weeks. The couple rented a sparsely furnished apartment, and Wagner hastily worked out the music for the second act of *Rienzi* on the same table where they ate their meals. He wanted to have something to show Meyerbeer when they finally met.

Near the end of August, Wagner was ready. He called on Meyerbeer, who graciously invited the younger man into his home. Wagner read from the libretto to *Rienzi* and Meyerbeer seemed impressed by his dramatic ability. He asked to see a copy of the score, and promised to introduce its author to the theater director at the Paris Opera, where Meyerbeer was the musical director. He also offered to supply Wagner with

Giacomo Meyerbeer. *(Courtesy of the Nissen Collection.)*

letters of introduction to several prominent musicians in both Boulogne and Paris. Wagner was elated, convinced he was on his way to stardom.

But things did not work out as Wagner had hoped. The Paris Opera eventually rejected *Rienzi,* saying it had the next seven years' worth of seasons already planned. The singers and conductors in Boulogne who invited Wagner to tea did so only as a courtesy to Meyerbeer—they had no reason to take on an unknown, impoverished German conductor. Wagner soon found there were two ways to be successful in France. He could buy his way in by paying for his own work to be performed, or he could work his way up from the bottom. But he was not rich enough, or patient enough, for either route.

Disillusioned, Wagner and Minna made their way to Paris, where they found an apartment in one of the poorer sections of town. They lived in a dismal building and were surrounded by struggling artists. Wagner befriended a few of these, in particular, a fifty-year-old bachelor named Anders who made music as a hobby, and an ailing scholar named Lehrs. Wagner spent most of his time with these men, concocting elaborate get-rich-quick schemes.

One such scheme involved writing songs in the French style for famous singers to perform in their concerts. Wagner was enthusiastic, hoping to break into elite musical circles. He wrote the music, and Anders and Lehrs contributed the words. Once they had completed a few pieces, Wagner met with every celebrity singer who would see him, then played the music for them. In general, the singers liked the songs, but not one expressed any interest in performing them. Wagner and his colleagues were complete unknowns, which meant they had no value at all in the socially conscious circles of Paris.

Frustrated, Wagner turned to Meyerbeer, who patiently listened to the young composer's ranting. When Wagner had exhausted himself, Meyerbeer gently suggested he try to

Richard and Minna's first residence in Paris.

break into the business from the ground floor. Wagner did not like the idea, but had so many bills to pay he was ready to try anything. Meyerbeer sent him to a publisher he knew named Schlesinger who made a good living publishing adaptations of operas and concert music for use in the home. He also published musical workbooks. From time to time, he would give Wagner an assignment to write a piano version of a popular opera or exercises for playing certain instruments. Wagner hated what he called "hack-work," but it kept him from debtor's prison.

In the meantime, however, his composing suffered and he fell into a depression. His spirits were lifted in the spring of 1840 when Meyerbeer came to Paris with good news. He introduced Wagner to his own personal agent, a man named Gouin. Wagner was bolstered by Meyerbeer's continued support when no one else recognized his talent, and thrilled when Gouin made arrangements to stage a full-scale production of *Das Liebesverbot* at the Renaissance Theater.

To celebrate what he was certain would be the first of many successes, Wagner immediately moved his wife into a larger apartment in a better neighborhood—the rent was put on credit, to be paid after the opera opened. But only a few days after he signed the lease, Wagner found out the theater had gone bankrupt. There would be no production, and certainly no money.

Wagner's old neighbor Lehrs intervened and tried to convince his friend that Meyerbeer had known all along the theater was going to close. He told Wagner that the older composer was threatened by his youth and talent and had set him up to fail. Initially, Wagner doubted Lehrs's accusations, but over time his bitterness grew. Eventually, Wagner came to hold Meyerbeer responsible for all his failures in Paris. That Meyerbeer was Jewish only fed Wagner's prejudices and further convinced him that Jews could not be trusted. He also began to adhere to the delusion of many anti-Semites—that Jews controlled everything through a secret organization that worked to keep him from being successful.

In the meantime, Wagner and Minna were broke. They could not afford to pay their rent. They sold what few possessions they had left, including her theatrical costumes. They pawned their wedding rings and rented out a room to a boarder, but still just barely scraped by. Wagner had to make more money. He continued to work for Schlesinger and, through him, met the editor of the *Gazette Musicale*. Wagner wrote a few articles for that paper, but half of that money

Wagner was able to supplement his meager income by writing for this newspaper.

went to an interpreter who helped him with his French.

In an effort to take his mind away from his problems, Wagner immersed himself in his music. He worked frantically, aware that he did not have much time before he would be ruined and have to leave Paris in disgrace. Wagner finished *Rienzi* and wrote the libretto for a one-act version of a popular ghost story called *Der Fliegande Holländer (The Flying Dutchman)*. The story told of a phantom sea captain cursed to roam the seas until a woman would rescue him with her love. If he was unable to sell a full-scale opera, Wagner hoped he could at least sell what was called a curtain-opener: a short theatrical work performed before the evening's main event. Once again, Meyerbeer interceded on Wagner's behalf. He introduced Wagner to the new manager of the Grand Opera, who read and liked the young composer's libretto. He said he only needed some time to determine whether he could fit a performance of it in.

While he waited for an answer, Wagner made the final notations on *Rienzi* in November of 1840. Rather than try to sell the piece to French musical directors who seemed uninterested in German work, Wagner sent the score to the grandest theater in Germany, the Dresden Royal Court Theater. It was a long shot, but the generous soprano Schröder-Devrient was singing there and Wagner hoped their friendship might help sway the directors in his favor.

As fall turned into winter, the Wagner finances looked grimmer. Finally, the couple decided they had no choice but

The Royal Court Theater in Dresden. *(Courtesy of Archiv für Kunst und Geschichte.)*

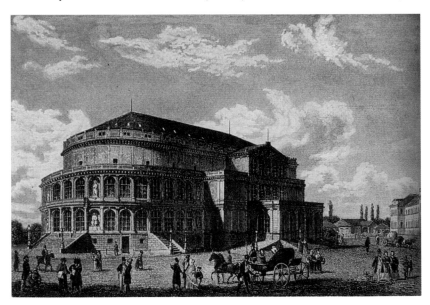

to return to Germany. Prospects in Paris did not look good. But when Wagner went to his landlord, on January 2, 1841, to end his lease, he found that he was a day too late. Leases turned over on January 1, and since Wagner had not notified his landlord of his intent to move, he was obligated for another year of rent. The composer protested, but to no avail. The expensive apartment was their responsibility for twelve more months.

The Wagners sublet their apartment and moved to a cheaper place outside of the city. Finally, their luck began to turn. Wagner's short pieces for the *Gazette Musicale* were becoming quite popular. The publisher asked for more stories, more money came in, and Wagner's name began to be known around Paris. The director of the Paris Opera liked what Wagner was doing, and decided to purchase the libretto for *The Flying Dutchman.* Naturally, Wagner asked to compose the music, as well, but the director wanted only the words. Wagner was caught between his dedication to his art and his need for money—the money won out.

It did not pay much, but it was enough to buy some time to compose without interruption. He began a full three-act version of *The Flying Dutchman,* which he intended to take back to Germany. He worked at an astonishing pace, completing the score in only seven weeks. His harrowing sea journey from Prussia to England served as inspiration for the tumultuous and dark first act. *The Flying Dutchman* stands as the first score written entirely in Wagner's own style, free from the influence of his studies.

In the fall of 1841, the people subletting the Wagner

**1ͭᵉ Vorstellung im vierten Abonnement.**

**Königlich Sächsisches Hoftheater.**

**Montag, den 2. Januar 1843.**

Zum ersten Male:

# Der fliegende Holländer.

Romantische Oper in drei Akten, von Richard Wagner.

**Personen:**

| | | | |
|---|---|---|---|
| Daland, norwegischer Seefahrer. | — | — | Herr Risse. |
| Senta, seine Tochter. | — | — | Mad. Schröder-Devrient. |
| Erik, ein Jäger. | — | — | Herr Reinhold |
| Mary, Haushälterin Dalands. | — | — | Mad. Wächter. |
| Der Steuermann Dalands. | — | — | Herr Bielezizky. |
| Der Holländer. | — | — | Herr Wächter. |

Matrosen des Norwegers. Die Mannschaft des fliegenden Holländers. Mädchen.

Scene: Die norwegische Küste.

Textbücher sind an der Casse das Exemplar für 2½ Neugroschen zu haben.

Playbill from an 1843 production of *The Flying Dutchman.*

apartment in Paris moved out and Wagner again needed to find the money for rent. When he could not, the landlord confiscated and sold all of their furniture. Wagner and Minna went back to Paris to live in their empty apartment and plan their next move. Before they could figure out what they were going to do, a near miracle occurred. Word came from Dresden that the Royal Court Theater would stage *Rienzi* and Schröder-Devrient would star.

Though the news was astounding, there was a downside. Wagner would not be paid in advance—and the show would not open until the fall of 1842. Because he could not afford to leave Paris, Wagner wrote literally hundreds of letters to the Dresden theater advising them on innumerable details of the production. Through the winter, he continued to

Wilhelmine Schröder-Devrient, the lovely and talented singer, was slated to star in the Dresden Royal Court Theater's production of Wagner's *Rienzi*. *(Courtesy of Historische Bildarchiv Handke.)*

scrape money together by writing articles for the *Gazette* and doing work for Schlesigner, but now his mind was focused on his music. He finished the longer version of *The Flying Dutchman,* and full of confidence, sent it off to the Berlin Theater. In March of 1842, they accepted it. Wagner was on his way.

When word reached his family that Richard was finally going to be a success, they collected some money to help him leave France. His Parisian acquaintances helped as well, and soon Wagner was able to pay off his landlord and some debts before leaving. "At last," Wagner wrote, "the hour of redemption came; the day arrived on which, as I devoutly hoped, I would be turning my back on Paris forever." After two and a half years, Wagner was going home.

# Chapter Four
## Success and Revolution

Wagner had not seen his family in the six years since he had married Minna. Most of them had long before written him off as a wastrel and a money pit and Wagner was eager to make amends. He went to Leipzig to see his mother and while there was able to convince the rest of the family that he was going to make something of himself after all. His brother-in-law even offered him a loan, which he would repay in installments over the next year. Johanna Wagner was proud of her son, and their only sadness was that Rosalie was no longer with them.

After Leipzig, Wagner went to Berlin to check in on the production plans for *The Flying Dutchman*. He was upset to find that the director who had accepted the opera was retiring, and the man taking his place, Karl Theodor von Kustner, had his own plans for the company. Wagner went back to Dresden uncertain whether *The Flying Dutchman* would be performed after all.

In Dresden, the company singers were on their summer holidays, so work was focused on the scenery, costume design, and orchestration for *Rienzi*. The musical director liked the opera but was concerned that it was too long—it ran over four hours. He wanted to make cuts, but Wagner refused to change a note. Finally, they reached a compromise that eliminated a half-hour long ballet sequence. The musical director wanted to cut still more, but Wagner made a point of being present at the theater every single day to prevent further changes. Wagner's presence was an irritant to the people trying to do their jobs, and some grumbled it would have been better for all concerned if he had remained in Paris.

When the rest of the company broke for summer vacation, and Wagner was satisfied nothing would be done in his absence, he returned to Berlin to talk to Kustner about *The Flying Dutchman.* Kustner was put off by the composer's aggression and told Wagner he was not sure he would be able to stage his work. The more he waffled, the harder Wagner pushed. The harder Wagner pushed, the more reluctant Kustner became to honor the word of the previous musical director. Discouraged and frustrated, Wagner returned to Dresden.

Things began to look up once the Dresden company returned from summer vacations and began rehearsals. Everyone involved loved the opera, including the lead tenor, Joseph Tichatschek, who was one of the most famous singers in the world. Wagner, ever difficult, was a little disappointed by Tichatschek's acting, but could find no fault with his voice. He was there for every rehearsal, and though money was still a problem, Wagner was happy.

*Rienzi* premiered on October 20, 1842. It started at 6:00 p.m. and the curtain did not come down until 11:30. Wagner was horrified to see audience members fidgeting in their seats and was convinced they would hate the production. He was wrong. The audience loved it, and the applause lasted past midnight. "No subsequent experience," Wagner wrote, "has given me feelings even remotely similar to those I had on this day of the first performance of *Rienzi*." Aristocrats came from all over Germany to see the new hit opera; Wagner's name was on everyone's lips. The success of *Rienzi* was such that the Dresden Royal Court Theater decided to stage *The Flying Dutchman*—the Berlin Opera had missed its chance.

*Rienzi* premiered in October 1842 in Dresden. Above, a scene from Act III. *(Courtesy of Deutsches Theatermuseum, Munich.)*

*The Flying Dutchman* premiered just after the New Year— and was a tremendous

Richard Wagner in an
1842 pencil drawing by
Ernst Benedikt Kietz.

disappointment. After the first performance, Wagner realized the problem lay in the difference between the opera he wrote and the kind of operas the singers were accustomed to performing. Most operas of the time were designed to show off the costumes and scenery. They had thin plot lines that served only to connect together the dazzling arias. Wagner was writing operas with deep and powerful storylines that needed strong actors to communicate the plot ideas. He realized that his operas would be successful only if he taught his singers an entirely new way of performing. From then on, he took it upon himself to direct his operas by getting on stage and doing their lines for them, asking them to copy his movements and gestures. He brought a new sensibility and refinement to the genre.

Before Wagner could totally revolutionize opera, his work would have to be performed in theaters across Europe. *The Flying Dutchman* closed after only four performances. *Rienzi* was revived, but the performances were too sporadic to bring in any real money. Wagner had hoped to live off of his income from his operas, but that was not to be. To make matters worse, as his name became more widely known throughout northern Europe, old creditors from Königsberg and Riga began to show up, certain that a famous composer would finally be able to pay off his debts. Schröder-Devrient gave Wagner a generous loan that covered his most pressing obligations, but it was not enough.

He applied for the position of *kapellmeister,* or court conductor, at the Dresden court. It was an excellent position, one that most musicians would be thrilled to have, with its steady income, prestige, and frequent association with nobility. Most kapellmeisters stayed in their posts their entire lives. But Wagner was not sure he wanted a job with such permanence. He worried that he would not have time for his own composing and would be kept too busy to supervise any further productions of his music.

Carl Maria von Weber, Wagner's childhood hero, had held the Dresden post until his death in 1826. Weber's widow met with Wagner and urged him to accept the job. She told him Weber would have wanted him to continue the work he had begun. On February 2, 1843, King Friedrich August II of Saxony officially offered Wagner the position, and the twenty-nine-year-old composer accepted.

Minna was thrilled that Wagner would finally have a

steady income and would be able to provide her with the stable middle-class life she desired. She was tired of running from debtors in the dark of night and watching Wagner lose composing jobs because he would not compromise his standards. What she did not realize was that all of his new income was going to pay old debts and that the new house and furniture he bought would, once again, be purchased on credit.

Despite his fears, Wagner did have time to give to his own work. On his thirtieth birthday, he finished an epic poem called "Der Venusberg," which would eventually become the libretto for the opera *Tannhäuser*. Wagner took the story from myth and wrote a beautiful opera about the knight Tannhäuser, who is torn between life with the seductive goddess Venus or returning to the mortal world. *Tannhäuser* concerns the themes of fate, free will, and love that characterize much of Wagner's work.

*The Flying Dutchman* had another chance when the Berlin Opera finally decided to stage it in March 1844. In order to avoid the failure of the Dresden performance, Wagner spent as much time as he could in Berlin training the actors and making sure rehearsals went as he wanted. This time, when *The Flying Dutchman* opened, it was a huge success. In the audience that night was the great composer and piano virtuoso Franz Liszt, one of the first musical superstars, whose piano playing and dashing good looks attracted huge audiences. Liszt was bowled over by the music and promised the young composer he would speak of him with the highest regard everywhere he went.

The Hungarian composer Franz Liszt was considered the greatest pianist of his time. He thrilled audiences with his flamboyant playing and good looks.

While Wagner continued to conduct for the court, he also worked to finish the score to *Tannhäuser.* It was to premiere in Dresden in 1845, and he still had to work out the orchestration (deciding which instruments would play which parts). *Tannhäuser* brought something new to opera—so new that Wagner would not even call it an opera. He referred to the piece as a musical drama and described its musical structure as one of "endless melody." He wanted to avoid the problem he had identified in the first failure of *The Flying Dutchman.* Instead of stringing together elaborate arias with a weak plot, he envisioned a continuous storyline, uninterrupted by applause. He wrote the score of *Tannhäuser* as if it were a symphony; the music was seamless, and matced the drama.

*Tannhäuser* had a lukewarm reception, however. Audiences were nonplussed by its novelty and uncertain as to what the composer was trying to achieve. They missed not having arias to applaud. One of the few who understood Wagner's innovations was a young critic, Eduard Hanslick. He wrote "If there is anyone among contemporary German composers from whom we can expect something distinguished in the field of serious grand opera, it is he. Richard Wagner is, I am convinced, the greatest dramatic talent among all contemporary composers." Hanslick's review helped, but Wagner would not get to read it for several months. In the meantime, he was frustrated by what he saw as audiences' inability to understand his work.

Wagner had long been fascinated by the ancient legend of Lohengrin, a knight of the Holy Grail (the cup from which Jesus drank at the Last Supper) who loves and marries a woman who does not know his true identity. The story had all the elements Wagner preferred—mystery, intrigue, heroism, love, and destiny. He felt compelled to set the story to music, and within a month's time, he had a libretto.

The winter of 1845-46 brought more financial problems for the Wagners. Richard's niece, Johanna, came to Dresden as a singer and actress. She had a remarkable voice and was very beautiful, and he cast her in *Tannhäuser.* This move angered his faithful soprano Schröder-Devrient, who

als, and a school where his ideas about musical drama could be taught seriously, not merely crammed into stolen moments in the middle of busy rehearsals. Conscious of the problems unhappy musicians and actors could make, he imagined a theater that paid artists well, and provided them with pensions for their old age. Finally, he pictured himself, the Royal Conductor, with complete control over all matters concerning the theater. Wagner outlined all of these ideas in a manifesto. But when he proposed the changes to the court, his ideas were rejected.

In February of 1848, as Wagner wondered what would become of his work, he received news that his mother had died. Johanna Wagner's death was a huge blow. She was the only living member of the family who consistently professed faith in him. He went to Leipzig for her funeral, aware that his last connection to the city had been severed. The rest of his family was spread over Germany and wanted little to do with the destitute composer. He had only Minna for company, and felt abandoned.

That same month saw radical political events that inaugurated great change in Europe. In France, the so-called February Revolution ousted King Louis Philippe in favor of a republican government. The effects of the coup rippled across the continent—people everywhere protested for freedom and the implementation of representative government. Within a month there were riots in all the major German cities. Several of the smaller states quickly fell to the revolts. In Dresden, King Friedrich August II tried to appease the rebels by firing his ministers and appointing more progressive, liberal leaders to their posts. Other rulers tried similar measures; instability plagued the region.

A group of rich, liberal intellectuals gathered in Frankfurt to try to bring the various states together. They thought the leaders were too weak to remain in power and hoped to seize the opportunity to unite Germany. They wanted to form a parliament and devise a constitution of laws. After eight months of deliberations, they offered the crown of all of Germany to Frederick III, King of Prussia.

The revolutionary spirit of 1848 made a deep impression on Wagner. He attended meetings, wrote pamphlets, and had a few radically leaning articles published. In June of 1848, he made a speech calling for "the downfall of the last glimmer of aristocratism…Further we want the unconditional right of voting and election to be granted to every adult person born in the country: the poorer he is the more he is in need of aid, the more natural is his claim to take part in drawing up the laws that are to protect him against poverty and need." He advocated for Saxony to remove its court officials and outmoded ideals but keep the king on his throne as a figurehead. His politics were somewhat self-serving: if the king vanished completely the court theater would collapse. However, he did want the country's wealth divided more equally among the people.

The speech Wagner made was quickly written and poorly worded, and when printed copies of it began to circulate, he was denounced as plotting to overthrow the government. Wagner had been misunderstood, but it was too late. All the productions of *Rienzi* planned for that month were cancelled, because the theater management was afraid there would be riots.

Insurrections were taking place all over the German-speaking world, including in Vienna, the capital of Austria. There was a violent battle between the revolutionaries and the Viennese army, but the rebellion was put down and the power was returned to the monarchy. The revolutionaries of Dresden returned to the streets and demanded that Saxony attack Austria.

Because of his support for the revolt, Wagner's *Lohengrin* premiere was cancelled. He spent all of his time conducting other composers' operas, and was feeling very frustrated. He began two new pieces, but no amount of writing could quell the "dull agitation" that grew in him that winter. But with spring came a pleasant surprise: Liszt wrote that he had just conducted two performances of *Tannhäuser* in Weimar, and hoped Wagner might come out for a third at the end of May. Wagner immediately asked for a leave of absence from Dresden, but before he was ready to go, the political situation came to a head.

The Frankfurt Parliament had offered the crown of Germany to Frederick III of Prussia. Because he refused to acknowledge that the Frankfurt Parliament had the authority to select a ruler, which would have been too democratic, Frederick III rejected their offer. Shortly thereafter, Friederich August II of Saxony also rejected the Frankfurt Parliament and democratic rule. On May 3, all the bells in Dresden were sounded, signaling the beginning of a revolt. The armory was attacked, and its guards fired a cannon into the crowd.

The city of Dresden, as painted by Bernardo Bellotto. *(Gemäldegalerie, Dresden.)*

Fighting broke out all over the city, and the Saxon king was forced into hiding until Prussian troops could arrive and quell the uprising.

Wagner was in full support of the revolution. He believed the German people needed to free themselves from the control of the elite in order to fully achieve their inherent greatness. His nationalistic sentiments favored a Germany run by its citizens, free from what he saw as the corrupting influences of foreigners and the nobility. This was part of his developing faith in the German *volk* (people), who he raised to a mythical level. Convinced that the only way German culture would be restored would be if the people were free to create, he blamed the elite and other groups, including the Jews, for conspiring against the *volk*. The core of his revolutionary impulses was mythical and nationalistic.

The rebels set up barricades around the city. Wagner ran back and forth between the town hall, where the rebel leaders met, and a tall church tower, from where he could see the fighting unfold. He threw himself into the conflict with unbridled enthusiasm. It was days before he could be persuaded to go home to check on Minna. She wanted to leave Dresden, so he packed her into a carriage and took her to stay with relatives in the neighboring town of Chemnitz. When he returned to Dresden, the revolution was over.

The Prussian army had overwhelmed the rebel forces. As he rode back into the city the army was breaking down barricades, searching houses, and rooting out the rebel leaders. Wagner learned that many had fled to an inn in Chemnitz, and he rushed to meet them. The Prussians got there first and arrested everyone present for treason. Wagner was a wanted man and needed to flee the country as quickly as he could.

Wagner was able to get to Weimar, where Franz Liszt, who had made arrangements to have Wagner smuggled out of the country, was waiting for him. Minna arrived in time to say goodbye, but they did not part on good terms. She was not a fugitive and so could stay behind in Dresden, and was angry that he had to leave her, despairing about what she would do alone.

Wagner was hidden in the theater so he could see a final rehearsal of *Tannhäuser*. Afterwards, he was given a fake passport and some money. He set out on a mail coach and then a steamer, all the time trying to conceal his thick Saxon accent. On May 28, he landed in Switzerland. He would not set foot in his beloved Germany for eleven years.

# Chapter Five
## From Exile to the Ring

Exile brought one happy surprise. Wagner discovered he was a celebrity in Switzerland. He was the guest of honor at dinner parties, where everyone praised *Rienzi* and *The Flying Dutchman* and looked forward to the Swiss premiere of *Tannhäuser.* Life in Zürich might not be as bad as he had anticipated after all.

Minna, though, was still unhappy. In anger, she wrote Wagner requesting a divorce, asking, "What sort of future do I face? What have you to offer me? I have no wish to dampen your courage; but to venture once again into the unknown, to court worries and misery in a foreign country, for this my courage is not enough. I have lost faith in your beautiful promises, and there is no longer any happiness for me on this earth!" Wagner told her to sell the Dresden house and furniture and keep the money: it was all he could offer her.

Though it had a terrible effect on his marriage, Zürich was a productive place for Wagner. He went straight to work. Instead of writing music, though, he wrote long philosophical essays outlining his beliefs. The first, "Art and Revolution," was published as a pamphlet. It explained his theory that art forms typically considered separate from each other—writing, music, acting, painting, sculpture, architecture—should be treated as one and made available to all people, not just the elite. Taking ancient Greece as his model, he argued that Greek theater was the ideal combination of the arts. The essay also called for the redistribution of wealth in order to create social parity, which is one tenet of socialism. The pamphlet sold well, and he began writing another, called "The Art-Work of the Future."

In August 1849, Wagner's work was interrupted when Minna appeared on his doorstep. He took her back, but soon regretted the reconciliation. He was happy in Switzerland, writing and planning to give talks about his ideas. But Minna expected to find him busy composing the opera that would make him a success in Paris. He had begun another opera, but had put it aside for a time. Minna pressured him until he finally returned to working on it. He wrote of that decision, "not only did I hate the idea, but I knew that I was doing an injustice to myself by believing in the success of my enterprise, for I felt that I could never seriously throw myself into it heart and soul."

In January of 1850, Wagner stood in line to buy a train ticket to Paris. He was so upset about the idea of going that he "felt . . . weak and broke out in . . . terrible perspiration."

His previous Parisian experiences had unsettled him so much that he could barely bring himself to board the train. Once again, Minna stayed behind until he could find the money to send for her.

Upon his arrival in Paris, Wagner found that nothing had changed. His operas were still not fashionable, his name had no cachet, his friends were still poor, and theater managers ignored him. "Deliverance from this hell," Wagner wrote, "is all I wish for." His deliverance came in the form of a rich, beautiful woman named Jessie Laussot.

Laussot had seen a performance of *Tannhäuser* several years previously and was a great admirer of Wagner's work. When she heard he was in Paris, she invited him to her house in Bordeaux. There Wagner was introduced to Laussot's friend Frau Ritter, and the two women offered him a generous loan to help him get on his feet financially. Wagner was amazed by their kindness, but even more taken by Laussot's beauty and her belief in him as an artist. They began an affair; she was already married, but they made plans to elope. Wagner wrote to Minna asking for a divorce.

Minna was furious. She borrowed money to travel to Paris. Hours before her arrival, Wagner learned she was on her way and fled to Geneva. From there, he planned to go to Greece, where Laussot would join him. Their plans were interrupted when Laussot's husband, who had discovered the affair, announced his intention to kill Richard Wagner.

Love affairs were nothing new for the Wagners, but this threat raised the drama of their marriage to new heights. Fortunately, crisis was averted when Frau Ritter's son, Karl

Paris as it looked in 1867. The city provided multiple challenges to Wagner and Minna, both monetarily and romantically. *(Courtesy of the Library of Congress.)*

Ritter, tracked Wagner down in Geneva. Ritter, an aspiring musician himself, was a devoted fan of Wagner's. He found his idol and relayed the news that Laussot's husband would not allow her to leave for Greece and that Minna had returned to Zürich. Wagner, afraid Laussot's husband would find him, could not go back to Paris. He swallowed his pride and returned to Minna. They reconciled, again.

A few months later, in August of 1850, Liszt conducted the premiere of Wagner's *Lohengrin* in Weimar. Wagner was frustrated not to be there. More than two years had passed since he completed the opera, and he still had not heard it performed with a full orchestra and chorus. The night of the performance, Wagner and Minna went to an inn for dinner, and imagined themselves in Weimar, as Wagner later recalled, by "marking the various times at which the performance presumably began, developed, and came to a close."

*Lohengrin*'s premiere marked a turning point in Wagner's career. For one thing, it proved that a Wagnerian opera could be performed in a small theater. Liszt's own popularity helped make *Lohengrin* fashionable, and small theaters throughout the territory rushed to add Wagner's operas to their repertoires. *Lohengrin* was also the opera that divided music lovers into pro- or anti-Wagner camps. Eduard Hanslick, the critic who had praised *Tannhäuser,* hated the new work. He wrote of the applause the opera received, "The general enthusiasm would in any case be more readily understood by a deaf person." Of Wagner's use of dramatic modulation, considered a brilliant innovation by some, Hanslick's review reported "In order to match every turn of dialogue with surprising musical coloration, he has recourse to perpetual modulation. I know of nothing so fatiguing as these half-recited songs in *Lohengrin* which never stay four measures in the same key."

Hanslick's review wounded Wagner and, though he was not the only critic to pan *Lohengrin,* the composer was especially offended by the review because Hanslick was Jewish. Wagner was still bitter over what he perceived as Meyerbeer's manipulation of him in Paris, and he could not see Hanslick's comments reasonably. He was convinced that Jews ran the music business, yet lacked the talent to truly appreciate music. He began to draft an article about the influence of Jews on music.

Minna and Wagner settled down in Zürich, finding a house that was not too expensive. Between the small amount of money Wagner made when his operas were performed and the stipend he still received from Frau Ritter, the couple managed to scrape by. Soon after they were settled, Karl Ritter came to stay with them. Wagner could hardly refuse the young man since his mother gave them so much money. Ritter wanted to be a musician, and Wagner agreed to help him find work. When the Zürich opera house wanted to hire Wagner to conduct, he offered them Ritter instead, saying he needed the time to work on his own compositions. They took Ritter on the condition that Wagner would substitute if Ritter could not handle the work.

To his despair, Wagner found Ritter was a terrible conductor. But before he took over conducting duties, he was saved by the arrival of Hans von Bülow. Twenty-year-old Bülow was an extremely talented pianist and conductor, and a great admirer of Wagner. He was happy to take over Ritter's duties at the podium for the chance to spend time with his hero. Ritter and Bülow became the first in a long line of men and women who believed Wagner's music and theories bordered on divine inspiration and would do anything to curry his favor. Hans von Bülow's time in Zürich was cut short when his parents insisted he go to Weimar, where they had arranged for him to study with Franz Liszt. Wagner was sorry to see the youth go, but knew Bülow would be in good hands.

During the winter of 1851-52, Wagner, now thirty-eight, devoted himself to writing a book called *Opera and Drama.* This would become one of his most notorious works. In it, he railed against the grand opera so popular at the time, saying it existed only to show off costumes and arias and neglected the drama he considered essential. Wagner also laid out his theories about what made good operas, and made a case for the kind of musical dramas he had been writing.

One of Wagner's most important assertions was that music should be subservient to the dramatic or emotional narrative of an opera. This flew in the face of traditional opera, where the beauty of the music was always more important that the plot—operas were routinely performed in languages foreign to the audience, who came to hear the music. Wagner also detailed his beliefs about the use of leitmotifs to represent feelings or characters, underscoring his claims that music should serve words, and not vice versa. These claims were significant not just for their oddity—few composers would argue that their music was less important than the words of the libretto—but also because, many years later, it would be revealed that Wagner did not actually believe what he said. He would one day confess that it was often the music that motivated his work, not the words.

The final element of *Opera and Drama* was its insistence that the only viable source for opera subjects was myth. Wagner believed that the repetition of heroic and inspiring stories from traditional German folklore could overcome the lethargy of the current culture, thus unlocking the inherent genius of the German people.

In this vein, Wagner began work on a new libretto he called *Siegfried's Death*. Adapted from mythology, the Siegfried legend describes a human hero who battles with gods, other humans, trolls, and dwarves for the possession of a magic ring which gives ultimate power to anyone wearing it. In the end, Siegfried brings the warring over the ring to an end, but only by sacrificing his life, as well as his wife's, to destroy the ring once and for all. (J.R.R. Tolkien was inspired in part by the Siegfried legend when he wrote *The Lord of the Rings* trilogy.)

*Siegfried's Death* was only the beginning of what would become a huge endeavor. Wagner had trouble composing the music to accompany the finished libretto until he decided he needed to tell the entire story—first narrating the history of the ring, then moving on to Siegfried's involvement, the story of his coming of age, and finally how he died in order to save the world from the destructive power of the ring. Each section of the story required its own opera. The *Ring* cycle, four complete operas, would take the rest of his career to finish. There was no theater in existence at that time that would agree to play four operas in a row, but Wagner was undeterred. He had a vision that would forever change the music world.

Liszt wanted to stage *Siegfried's Death* as soon as possible and pressured Wagner to finish the music. The stress made Wagner break out in hives and he and Minna went to a spa in the country for a rest. While there, Wagner first read the newspaper *Neue Zeitschrift für Musik,* a periodical dedicated to modern music. It was published by Franz Brendel, who shared many of Wagner's personal and political views. Wagner sent Brendel a copy of the article he had written about Jews in music, and Brendel published it.

"Judaism in Music" charged that Jews were materialistic

and kept German art and culture from excelling. Wagner felt that Germans should celebrate German culture, and he bemoaned the fact that so much of their art, architecture, fashion, and music came from Italy or France. The problem, Wagner believed, was that too many people of Jewish descent lived in German cities and towns. Economic and political changes meant that many Jews left their homes in eastern Europe and moved westward. Wagner claimed that Jews had no cultural history of their own and that their influence was weakening the culture of Germany. He called for all Jews to be eliminated from German music and culture.

The article was published under a pseudonym, *Freigedank*—German for freethinker—but there was little doubt about the author's true identity. Wagner never denied writing the piece, and as it circulated, the division between Wagnerites and anti-Wagnerites deepened. Many of Wagner's former supporters left him, but his anti-Semitic comments, unfortunately, found many sympathetic ears.

Brendel and his newspaper continued to support Wagner, and dubbed the kind of music Wagner and Liszt made the "music of the future." Liszt formed a group of composers, conductors, and virtuoso musicians that became known as the New German School. They stood in opposition to musicians like Robert Schumann and, later, Johannes Brahms, who wrote traditional music in the style of Felix Mendelssohn and Johann Sebastian Bach. Brahms and Schumann coined the term *absolute music* to describe their preference for music that stood alone, uncomplicated by poetic or visual elements. Wagner did not throw himself into the controversy with the same intensity as Liszt, but he provided many of the New German School's ideas, and he was branded an enemy of absolute music.

Over the course of 1852, Wagner worked on the libretto for the Siegfried legend, which is commonly referred to as Wagner's *Ring* cycle. The first opera in the cycle is *Das Rheingold,* which explains the origin of the ring. The next is *Die Walküre,* which explains the history of the ring and Siegfried's parentage. The third, and shortest, is *Siegfried,* and the fourth is *Götterdämmerung, or The Twilight of the Gods.* These last two follow the story of the ring to its inevitable conclusion. The *Ring* cycle is remarkable in its scope and its characters—from Wotan, king of the Gods, to the siblings Sieglinde and Siegmund, who are also the parents of the hero Siegfried, to the famous Valkyries, and the countless dwarves and lesser gods who inhabit Wagner's mythical world.

During this time, Wagner found financial support from admirers. Chief among them were Otto and Mathilde Wesendonck who had made a fortune in the silk trade. Their generosity supported the composer as he worked on the *Ring* cycle. Wagner

Mathilde Wesendonck. *(Richard Wagner Museum, Bayreuth.)*

began an affair with Mathilde Wesendonck that could end his livelihood if her husband discovered it. But, driven by passion, Wagner could not restrain his desires.

To escape the tense situation, Wagner left Minna in Zürich and went to Italy for the summer. He kept busy leading concerts and writing articles and poems, but he was not composing. He was both anxious and terrified to approach the *Ring* cycle, and later described his feelings: "I still felt the peculiar disinclination and fear of taking up composing again that I had previously experienced after protracted pauses in musical production. I also felt very much exhausted by all I had done and gone through, and the ever-recurring longing to break completely with everything in the past." He hoped Italy would be inspiring.

After three months in a small coastal town, Wagner began to hear the opening music to thr *Ring*. In a famous passage from his autobiography, he wrote:

> I suddenly had the feeling of being immersed in rapidly flowing water. Its rushing soon resolved, resounding in persistent broken chords; these in turn transformed themselves into melodic figurations of increasing motion, yet the E-flat major triad never changed, and seemed by its continuance to impart infinite significance to the element in which I was sinking. I awoke in sudden terror from this trance, feeling as though the waves were crashing high above my head. I recognized at once the orchestral prelude to *Das Rheingold*…had at last been revealed."

He returned to Zürich to get to work.

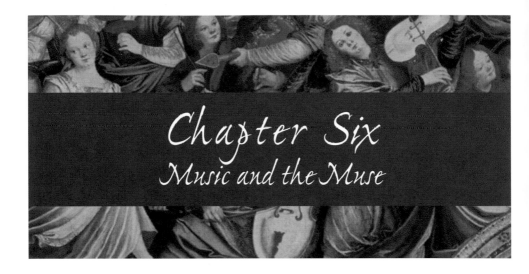

# Chapter Six
## Music and the Muse

In Zürich, Wagner wrote furiously. He finished the score for *Das Rheingold* in less than a year and, by the end of 1854, had finished the second opera in the series, *Die Walküre*. In January of 1855 he was invited to conduct a series of concerts with the London Philharmonic. The four-month appointment seemed like a much-needed break from the frenzy of composition, and he agreed to go. He had never been to England, and the prospect of travel appealed to him.

London, though, turned out to be a disappointment. Wagner was not a popular figure there. His essay "Judaism in Music" had been poorly received, and English critics were not predisposed to review him positively. The London Philharmonic Society pleaded with the composer to do something to appease the critics, but he steadfastly refused. The concerts were not a success, and Wagner later wrote

"…the society began…to regret my appointment, realizing that they had an entirely intractable and pig-headed person to deal with." Wagner went through the motions of his commitment, but wanted only to return to Switzerland.

Once back home, Wagner fell ill, and it was not until the beginning of 1857 that he was able to return his attention to composing. The Wesendoncks offered him the use of a cottage on Lake Lucerne, where he could write in peace. Minna went with him, mainly to put herself between him and Mathilde. They moved in on April 20.

Over the summer, Wagner stopped work on *Siegfried*. He was disappointed that publishers were not offering him more money for the *Ring* cycle. They did not believe it would ever be performed. The operas were too long and too challenging. Wagner believed deeply in his work, but turned away from it in frustration. He would not take it up again for another seven years.

While at Lake Lucerne, Wagner read *The World as Will and Idea* by the philosopher Arthur Schopenhauer, who was highly influential in artistic circles. Schopenhauer wrote that all living things are slaves to their own wills, and that this will leads us to want what we cannot have. For Schopenhauer, the only escape from this miserable situation was death. Self-inflicted death was not an option, however, because suicide was itself an expression of will. According to this philosophy, one merely has to endure life until its suffering is over. Wagner was captivated by Schopenhauer's philosophy, which articulated the themes implicit in his own musical dramas.

The cottage on Lake Lucerne was a constant reminder of Mathilde. Wagner had come to consider her his muse, and believed it was only by thinking about her that he could compose. Because of Minna's presence and Mathilde's husband, the lovers were rarely together. Wagner considered himself to be proof of Schopenhauer's theory that desire

Arthur Schopenhauer.

leads to suffering, and he began work on a new opera that would combine Schopenhauer's beliefs with his own experiences.

The story of *Tristan and Isolde* is an old romance, first put down by a German poet, Gottfried of Strasburg, in the thirteenth century. It is the tragic tale of Tristan, a knight who is escorting a princess, Isolde, to the castle where she will marry his king. On the journey, the two fall in love. Believing their love to be wrong, neither dares to tell the other. They are tricked into drinking a love potion, which intensifies their feelings and leads to a revelation. They decide to run away together, but this only leads to their death. The story illustrates Schopenhauer's conviction that desire leads to suffering and that the only escape from a life of pain is death. It also symbolizes Wagner's frustrated longing for Mathilde.

Once the libretto for the first act of *Tristan and Isolde*

was finished, the Wagners had their first guests of the summer. Hans von Bülow was on his honeymoon and brought his new wife to meet his hero. Wagner invited the couple to stay. He was delighted to see Bülow, and was instantly taken with his young wife, Cosima.

Cosima von Bülow was the illegitimate daughter of Franz Liszt and the French writer Marie d'Agould. She had been staying with her father when Bülow came to study, and she fell in love with him the night he conducted a performance of Wagner's *Tannhäuser*. The audience booed and hissed the performance so much that Bülow fainted from the stress. Cosima pledged herself to a man who felt his art so deeply. Two years later, they were married. Only a few weeks later, though, she realized the marriage was a mistake and that she was passionately in love with Richard Wagner. In the evenings, she would weep as Wagner read his poetry. Her husband thought she was moved by the words and never imagined that she had begun to think about suicide. Wagner was not oblivious to the young woman's feelings, but the Bülows went on their way before anything happened between them.

By the spring of 1858 Wagner had finished the *Tristan and Isolde* libretto as well as the music for the first act. He had arranged to sell the publishing rights and was hurrying to finish the music when his domestic life erupted. Minna found a love letter Wagner had written to Mathilde. When she confronted him, he denied it. Minna was furious; she knew the truth. She confronted first Mathilde and then Otto Wesendonck, who rushed his wife away for an extended stay

Cosima von Bülow and her father, Franz Liszt.

in Italy. Wagner was furious with Minna, afraid that Otto Wesendonck would evict him from the cottage and cut off his allowance. He told Minna he would divorce her if Wesendonck cut off their stipend. Minna left for a spa in Germany, where she stayed for three months. Wagner was alone, and desperate to finish *Tristan and Isolde.*

Minna came back at the end of the summer but little had changed. The Wesendoncks asked the Wagners to leave, and Wagner left his wife behind. On August 17, he made plans to travel to Venice without her. He later wrote "I remember that I never once looked back, or shed a tear on taking leave of her, and this almost terrified me."

Determined to finish *Tristan,* Wagner took rooms in Venice and went to work. His few distractions from composing were attending concerts and writing—each day he recorded his love for and devotion to Mathilde in a diary he kept for her, though she never saw it. He also wrote to Minna, who was living with relatives in Dresden. He was delighted to see a local performance of *Lohengrin*—the first time Venice had put on an entire Wagner opera. Though he was pleased, most of Venice was unimpressed and the critic Hanslick gave him yet another bad review. Wagner continued to push to have his work produced as he was in desperate need of the royalties. He was supporting two households and the little he earned from small productions of his operas was not enough to pay his bills.

*Tristan* was finally finished in March 1859, just as war broke out. Venice had long been controlled by Austria and was determined to be free. Afraid of being trapped in the city, Wagner fled back to Lake Lucerne, where he was embarrassed to encounter the Wesendoncks. But the tension between them had passed. Otto Wesendonck even gave Wagner a good deal of money—the equivalent of what a publisher would pay—for the rights to the *Ring* operas. He was certain they would be worth a lot some day.

Unable to return to Germany, and with Italy and Austria in chaos, Wagner decided he would make another attempt to live in France. He wrote to Minna and invited her to join him there. In the fall of 1859, the reunited couple took up residence in Paris again. This time, Wagner believed he was going to be a success. Instead of begging music directors to produce his operas, he would put on his own concerts. The first one, in January of 1860, had an enthusiastic audience, but was panned by the French critics. He was not entirely surprised, since his music was so closely tied to his German nationalist feelings. Trying another tactic, he wrote directly to Napoleon III, and asked for permission to perform at the Paris Opera.

The emperor did not respond, but Princess Metternich of Austria did. She was a great fan of Wagner's work, and close friends with the empress of France. Together, the women insisted that the emperor command a performance of *Tannhäuser* at the Paris Opera. The directors were angry that Wagner had managed to circumvent their authority, and even Wagner worried that a performance of *Tannhäuser* was not a good idea. It would have to be translated into French and, in order to appeal to French audiences, a grand ballet would have to be added to the second act. What concerned him most was that he would not be allowed to conduct.

Princess Metternich urged Wagner to take advantage of the opportunity to have his opera performed on the grandest stage in Paris. She also promised to go to Saxony on his behalf to ask for amnesty so he could return. Wagner was so grateful he could not refuse her. The princess did find Wagner amnesty in every German territory—except Saxony—and plans for *Tannhäuser* went ahead.

There were problems from the very beginning. It took

several tries before Wagner found someone to do a satisfactory translation of the libretto. He added some music to stretch out a short ballet sequence in the opening scene, but refused to indulge the Parisian taste for a grand ballet, saying it would ruin the story. Wagner was, as was his habit, very involved in the rehearsal process, but had difficulty convincing the singers to act the way he wanted them to. The conductor was not to Wagner's liking, and he was convinced his score was being slowly and painfully destroyed.

The first performance, in March of 1861, was a disaster. A group of aristocratic men who called themselves the Jockey Club attended operas primarily to see the beautiful dancers who performed the second act ballet. When they learned there would be no ballet in this opera, they smuggled in horns, bells, and whistles. In the middle of the first act they began to yell and make as much noise as they could. Wagner's fans responded by yelling back, and soon the din was unbearable. Bravely, the conductor and the singers kept the performance going, even though they could not hear the music.

After such a disastorous premiere, Wagner begged for the rest of the performances to be cancelled. His requests were denied—the opera house managers were delighted by the excitement. News of the protests was everywhere, and street vendors were selling "Wagner whistles" outside the opera house. After several more similar performances, the opera was finally withdrawn. Wagner had failed in France yet again. It was time to return to Germany.

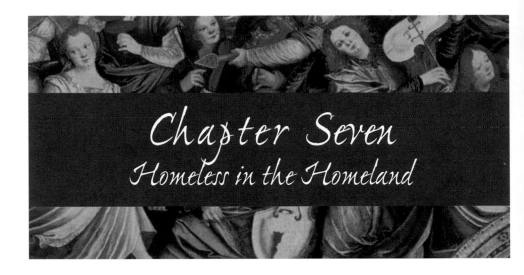

# Chapter Seven
## Homeless in the Homeland

Wagner's failure in Paris made him anxious for a new start. He planned to make Vienna his new "base of operations," and insisted that Minna go back to Dresden, alone. He considered their marriage to be over, though he did not tell Minna for fear of causing another terrible fight. She went back to Germany, believing her husband would join her there soon.

Vienna welcomed Wagner with open arms. The rulers forgave him his support of the 1848 rebellion and he was honored as a musical hero. Productions of *The Flying Dutchman* and *Lohengrin* were mounted. Plans were made to put up *Tristan and Isolde,* but the lead tenor lost his voice, and the production had to be delayed. Rumors quickly swirled that Wagner's production was cursed, and Wagner was frustrated at yet another obstacle on his road to success.

While waiting for *Tristan* to be played, Wagner was inspired to write a new opera called *Die Meistersinger,* or *The Mastersingers.* Though not based in myth or folklore, it was still distinctively German. Set in the sixteenth century, the story centers around an old ritual in which craftsmen gather in the town of Nuremberg to hold singing contests. The hero is a young knight, Walter, who wants to win the contest and with it the love of the beautiful Eva. Assisted by a cobbler and song master named Hans Sachs, the knight succeeds.

As much as he wanted to dedicate himself to composing, Wagner still had to find a way to pay his bills. He went to a publisher, Franz Schott, and asked for a large advance in exchange for the rights to *Die Meistersinger.* Schott initially refused, then agreed to give Wagner the money in small

Vienna, Austria, one of the primary centers of Western music. Wagner was treated like a hero there. *(Courtesy of Malvisi Archive, Populonia.)*

Princess Metternich.
*(Courtesy of Historische Bildarchiv Handke.)*

installments over the time it would take him to finish the new opera. Now that he had some money, Wagner needed a place to live. Princess Metternich offered him rooms in Paris, and despite his loathing for that city, Wagner could not turn down free—and luxurious—lodging. He headed back west.

He arrived in Paris to discover that the princess's offer had fallen through, which meant he would have to pay for his own room. Despite this setback, his work went well and, as Wagner wrote, "my *Meistersinger* poem swelled daily as the couplets flooded in. How could I help being put in a good humor?" He stayed in Paris through January, when the full libretto was finished, then returned to Germany.

Once again, Wagner found himself homeless. He tapped all of his regular sources for housing or money and found little forthcoming. His previously generous benefactors were disillusioned by Wagner's tendency to spend the money they gave him on extravagant houses and furnishings and then ask for help with daily expenses. But Wagner was convinced he could not work unless he had fine clothes, a grand piano, and all the trappings of an elegant lifestyle. He could not understand why his supports would deny him these things. He wrote to Liszt:

> Good Gracious! . . . such sums as I might *earn* . . . people ought to *give* me, without asking anything in return beyond what I am actually doing, and which is the best that I can do. Besides this, I am much better adapted to spend sixty thousand francs in six months than to "earn" it. The latter I cannot do at all, for it is not my business to "earn" money, but it is the business of my admirers to give me as much money as I want, to do my work in a cheerful mood.

When Wagner finally found a place to live, an apartment in the German town of Biebrich with a lovely view of the Rhine river, he had his belongings shipped from Paris. Minna came for a ten-day visit to reclaim the pieces that meant the most to her. She brought Wagner news that the king of Saxony had finally relented and would allow him to return. Their home in Dresden would be there whenever he was ready to come back. Early in her visit, Wagner seemed to consider the possibility of once more reuniting with Minna. But their fighting quickly resumed, and when Minna left for Dresden, the couple parted for the last time.

For the next year, Wagner continued to live a peripatetic lifestyle. He struggled to get his operas performed, then backed out when directors wanted to make changes he did not approve of. He was shunned by audiences critical of the New German School's musical style, and applauded heartily by those who supported it. He made some money, but spent it just as quickly.

In the fall of 1864, Hans von Bülow invited Wagner to Berlin. Wagner was happy to go. Cosima had recently had a baby girl, and the Bülow household was cheerful. Wagner spoiled the baby with attention and enjoyed time with his old friends. Then one day, while Hans was out, Cosima and Wagner went for a carriage ride, alone. "In time," Wagner wrote, "our jesting died away in silence. We gazed speechless into each other's eyes; an intense longing for an avowal of the truth overpowered us and led to a confession, which needed no words, of the boundless unhappiness that weighed upon us. With tears and sobs, we sealed our confession to belong to each other alone." Wagner had fallen in love with the wife of his best friend and most loyal supporter.

This affair was not easy for Wagner. He did not want to hurt Bülow. He left Berlin as soon as he could, and was once again on the move. Creditors hounded him and his landlord sold his furniture without warning. Afraid of being arrested, Wagner roamed until he found a friend in Munich, the capital of Bavaria, who was willing to take him in. He was angry, resentful, broke, and lonely—the fifty-year-old composer must have been an unpleasant houseguest. He wrote to a friend in despair: "Only a miracle can save me now."

It was then, when Wagner seemed to be at his lowest, that something happened to raise him back up. The relief appeared in the form of King Ludwig II, the eighteen-year-old ruler of Bavaria. Ludwig II was a fan of Wagner's work. He had his own copy of the libretto of the *Ring* cycle. Wagner

King Ludwig II of Bavaria. *(Courtesy of Süddeutscher Verlag, Bildarchiv.)*

had written a preface to the libretto acknowledging that it was too big for any theater to produce, and then boldly adding:

> It would on the other hand be very easy for a German prince [to produce], who would not have to make any new charge on his budget for this end but would simply have to make use only of those means that hitherto had been allocated to maintain the worst public institute of art, his opera house that so deeply compromises and corrupts the musical intelligence of the Germans. . . . Will such a prince be found?

Ludwig decided that he was that prince and, as soon as he took the throne, sent for Wagner. The search was difficult because Wagner was on the run from his creditors, but the composer was eventually located in Switzerland.

When the king's men arrived, Wagner took them for agents of his creditors trying to trick him. He did not believe that the secretary to the king of Bavaria would want anything to do with him. When the secretary himself showed up Wagner was nowhere to be found. The secretary persevered until he caught Wagner at home, then persuaded him there was no trick. Flabbergasted, Wagner agreed to leave for Munich after lunch.

King Ludwig II was young, dreamy, idealistic, and impulsive. Later in life, he would come to be known as the mad king. He had fairy-tale castles constructed throughout his kingdom, and took midnight sleigh rides in the Alps. He once made a cabinet member dress up as the Swan Knight from *Lohengrin*. The two of them rode in a boat pulled by swans in the moat around his castle for two consecutive nights while an orchestra on the bank played Wagner's music.

Ludwig and Wagner became close friends. They spent hours discussing philosophy, politics, and music. Though Wagner was old enough to be the king's father, they had much in common. Ludwig finally freed Wagner from the financial problems that had plagued him his entire career. He paid off his debts, gave him a place to live, and provided him with a generous salary. All he asked in return was Wagner's company and his music. Wagner had no official duties, and if he could live within the generous boundaries of the king's indulgence, he would have the creative freedom he had sought for years.

# Chapter Eight
## The King

King Ludwig II gave Wagner a virtually unlimited line of credit, and Wagner was not timid about using it. He had every wall of his house, including the ceiling, lined with pink satin. He ordered expensive French perfumes to fill the air and had his clothes made of the finest silk. Each day, Ludwig sent a carriage that would bring Wagner to the castle to spend hours with his patron. He promised the king performances of *Tristan, Meistersinger,* and the *Ring* cycle, plus two new operas. Although Ludwig paid well up front, he retained all the rights to Wagner's works. As owner of the operas, the king could control when and where they were produced.

In order to do his best work, Wagner told Ludwig he needed Hans von Bülow at the court. When he could not come right away, Bülow sent Cosima. For eight weeks,

Cosima and Wagner conducted a passionate love affair that resulted in a pregnancy. For more than fifty years, their child was passed off as Hans's daughter.

Officials at court and members of the Munich artistic community soon learned of Wagner's excessive spending habits, and began a campaign to have him removed. The more money he spent, the less was available to them. The local newspapers thought Wagner was making a fool of the king and printed full-page satirical caricatures of him. Rumors about his relationship with Cosima swirled.

Both King Ludwig and Bülow turned a blind eye to the affair. Ludwig refused to believe his favorite composer could make him a fool, and Bülow was completely under Wagner's spell. He believed the world should "venerate [Wagner] like a God," and was willing to sacrifice his own happiness to that end. Though the rest of the world could see Wagner's faults, his closest supporters remained faithful.

In December of 1864, Wagner conducted a performance of *The Flying Dutchman*. The music went well, but he was disappointed by the scenery and staging. He pressed Ludwig to build him a theater and Ludwig agreed. Planning began at once. Wagner was given complete freedom over the design. What he proposed looked like a modern theater— a flat stage (as opposed to the thrust-out stages of the day), an audience that faced the stage from a distance, to allow a wider perspective, and a pit for the orchestra beneath the stage so the musicians could be heard but not seen.

Ludwig's court thought the theater construction was a

waste of money and lobbied to stop it. They argued that Wagner's operas had been performed successfully all over Europe—there was no need for a special theater. There were also those who thought the design would ruin the theater-going experience. The controversy raged, but Wagner would not back down. When the cabinet members realized the theater would not go away, they turned their efforts to removing Wagner himself.

Though he knew he had enemies, Wagner was confident Ludwig would never abandon him. He flaunted his position and power in the court, even publicly patronizing the king. At home, he resumed work on *Siegfried* and planned to start the music school he had long envisioned that would be dedicated to teaching his approach to singing and playing music. He also worked to prepare *Tristan and Isolde* for its world premiere, in May of 1865.

*Tristan* created more animosity in Ludwig's court. Wagner insisted that Bülow conduct, and sent for singers from Dresden to star. Ludwig and Malvina Schnorr, who he insisted appear in the title roles, were world-renowned performers and did not work cheaply. They also took jobs away from court musicians, who feared Wagner was determined to replace them all. As the opera went into rehearsals, Cosima gave birth to what most people guessed was Wagner's child, a daughter Cosima promptly named Isolde.

Wagner had been waiting to see *Tristan* performed for ten years, and it seemed as if it might never happen. When the day of the opening finally arrived, Wagner's fears were confirmed. Bailiffs arrived at his doorstep to seize furniture and his piano as payment of a five-year-old debt from Paris. Wagner had to beg the court for an emergency loan, which was reluctantly granted. When Cosima went to pick up the money, it was given to her in small coins—a deliberate insult. She had to hire two carriages to cart the bags. Then the news came that Malvina Schnorr had lost her voice, and the opera had to be postponed.

Rumors that *Tristan* was cursed began to circulate again. The press speculated that Wagner had ruined Malvina with his impossible music. People whispered that Bülow had stage fright and that the orchestra was on strike. By the time Malvina was ready to sing, a full month later, the buzz surrounding the opera had died down and the audience was much smaller than it would have been. The opera opened and continued to play until the lead tenor, Ludwig Schnorr, unexpectedly died. It was rheumatism, not Wagner's music, that killed Schnorr, but his death gave new life to old rumors and did little to improve Wagner's reputation. *Tristan* was taken off the stage.

King Ludwig suggested to Wagner that he write his autobiography. Wagner was quite taken by the idea of seeing his entire life in print, and set about writing *Mien Leiben,* or *My Life,* which he dedicated to Cosima. Wagner's autobiography is not totally honest—it underplays his love affairs, his financial problems, and his involvement in the revolution of 1848—but it does offer insight into what is undeniably an interesting life.

As he was writing his autobiography, Wagner also kept a diary of thoughts he wanted to share with the king. In it, he detailed his views on German culture and politics. Members of the court suspected that Wagner was influencing the king, but had no proof until his diary was made public in a Munich newspaper under the title "What is German?" This was all the cabinet needed to convince themselves that the composer was poisoning the king with his controversial political ideas. Wagner retaliated with an article calling for the resignation of the entire court, and the court countered by accusing the king of condoning Wagner's adulterous affair with Cosima von Bülow. The king could not afford an insurrection, so Wagner was sent away.

Though his exile from Munich was supposed to last only six months, Wagner left in December of 1865 convinced he would never return. The king promised to continue to provide his composer with a comfortable allowance. Wagner needed only to find a place to live. He tried a few weeks in the frigid winter of Switzerland, then moved to the sunny French Riviera, where he hoped to focus on finishing *Die Meistersinger*.

The Munich press continued to attack Wagner, publishing an article that implied he had left Minna penniless in Dresden while he frolicked in luxury with Cosima. Minna was very ill, and Hans von Bülow went to Dresden to see her. While he was there, she composed a letter to the Munich newspaper saying she had "received sufficient support from my absent husband, Richard Wagner, to live a decent life, free from care." A few weeks later, Minna died. Wagner asked Bülow to arrange the funeral, which he himself did not attend.

In the spring of 1866, Wagner invited Cosima and her

Cosima

daughters to Lake Lucerne for a vacation. Hans was busy with a concert tour. Wagner was so inspired by Cosima's presence that he easily finished the music for the first act of *Die Meistersinger.* Meanwhile, Cosima became pregnant with their second child. Wagner found a house with a beautiful view of the Alps; he wanted Cosima and their children to stay there with him. The only way this could be accomplished was if Hans came too, so the entire Bülow family came to live with Wagner for the summer in the house he called Triebschen.

As if this living situation was not unusual enough, King Ludwig wrote from Bavaria that he wanted to surrender his throne to come to live with Wagner. "So long as I am King I cannot be united with him: the stars are against us," he wrote, and went on to say, "my place is with him; destiny

Wagner's house, Triebschen, perches in the cluster of trees at the center of this painting of Lake Lucerne. *(Courtesy of Richard Wagner Museum, Bayreuth.)*

calls me to his side." Wagner was alarmed by the king's intention, both because he depended on the king for money and because Bavaria was about to go to war with Prussia. Bavaria was aligned with the Austrian Empire, which in June of 1866 would declare war on Prussia in an attempt to stop the unification of Germany. Bavaria would be caught in the crossfire between Prussia and Austria, and King Ludwig would be lucky to maintain his power by the time the fighting was through. For his own sake, Wagner hoped that Ludwig could do so.

Wagner wrote to the king with his concerns, but Ludwig sneaked away from Munich and arrived at Triebschen in time to celebrate Wagner's fifty-third birthday. Cosima and Wagner begged him to return to Bavaria, but it was too

Hans von Bülow

late—the papers had found out about his escape and King Ludwig was ridiculed. One article, which accused Ludwig of turning a blind eye to Wagner and Cosima's affair, upset Hans so much that he challenged the journalist to a duel. By now, Bülow knew the truth. As he wrote to a friend, "Since February of 1865 I was not in the least doubt of the rottenness of things," but he had done his best to avoid admitting it.

The situation was out of hand, and Wagner had to do something. He needed the support of Bülow, who he hoped would run his new music school in Bavaria. He needed the king to retain his throne so he could continue to support Wagner and finance his operas. Wagner wrote a letter, full of lies, that swore he and Cosima were innocent of adultery and that Hans should be excused for his feud with the reporter. The king signed the letter, but it took a war to distract the public from the drama that was Richard Wagner's life.

In May of 1866, Austria and Prussia went to war to determine which state would control the German territories.

The prime minister of Prussia, Otto von Bismarck, had wide popular support and a strong, industrial economy to draw upon. Prussia boasted five railway lines and the more modern weaponry. Austria had been weakened by recent wars, and on July 3, the seven-week war ended with the worst defeat in Austrian history. Bismarck allowed Austria's ally Bavaria to keep its independence in return for paying heavy taxes and ceding some territory to Prussia. Ludwig stayed in power, but all of his court ministers were replaced.

Now that Wagner's enemies at court were gone, he could have returned to Munich. But he was happy at Lake Lucerne, and did not want to leave Cosima and their new daughter, Eva Maria (named after a character in *Meistersinger*). Hans had moved out of Wagner's home, but remained nearby.

Ludwig wanted more productions of Wagner's operas in Munich, but Wagner would only agree if Bülow could be brought in to conduct them and named director of the new music school. Ludwig appointed Bülow to the position of court kapellmeister, the highest-ranking musical job in the country. He would be offered "a further post with a fixed salary" when the music school opened. The only condition was that Bülow had to move back to Munich and Cosima had to come with him. Everyone was fooled into believing the affair had finally come to an end, and the Bülows certainly gave a good show of being back together. On October 1, the music school opened. Hans ran all the operations and oversaw new productions of *Lohengrin* and *Tannhäuser*.

Ludwig was beside himself with excitement when he

Wagner and his daughter Eva Maria.

learned that *Die Meistersinger* was ready to be staged. He arranged for the premiere of this new opera to take place in June of 1868. The king had also funded a small newspaper to publish Wagner's writings and news about events at the music school. Wagner wrote a series of fifteen articles for the newspaper called "German Art and German Politics," which announced that for Germany to have its own claim to art, it must rid itself of outside influences, namely the Jews and the French. He also reissued his "Judaism in Music." These articles stirred the press throughout Europe into action again, and people who had forgiven him for his article of 1850 were not so willing to look the other way this time. Even Queen Victoria of Britain called Wagner's writing "truly cracked."

Ludwig was horrified by what Wagner was writing. Although the king shared many of Wagner's views, he thought he should be diplomatic and choose his words wisely. He stopped the newspaper from publishing any more of Wagner's work and then tried to distance himself from Wagner's claims by publicly stating that "all men are brothers whatever their religion."

On June 21, 1868, *Die Meistersinger* had its premiere. Despite the fact that some audience members booed and hissed at the beginning of the evening, it was by far Wagner's greatest triumph to date. He nearly ruined his fine moment by standing to accept his applause from where he sat with King Ludwig in the Royal Box, as if he were royalty himself. This presumptuous behavior led to some unkind reviews and reignited rumors about his affair with Cosima.

Wagner tried once more to convince the king that the rumors were false, but to no avail. Ludwig finally realized that Wagner had been using him, and refused to answer any of his letters. When Cosima asked her husband for a divorce, the truth of the situation became undeniable. Hans von

Bülow refused to grant the divorce, but Cosima moved out and did not see him again for eleven years. Hans, humiliated, resigned from his job in Munich and fled the country.

Cosima came to live with Wagner on a permanent basis. She gave birth to a baby boy, named Siegfried, the following June. That summer the couple met a young professor of philosophy, Friedrich Nietzsche. This devoted Wagnerite was only twenty-four, but he shared an interest in the writings of Schopenhauer, and through many deep conversations about art and philosophy they became close. Nietzsche was soon a regular visitor at Triebschen.

Wagner's powerful self-assuredness influenced Nietzche's early philosophic work. To Nietzsche, Richard Wagner was the ideal man of the Romantic era: creative, independent and fiercely nationalistic. Yet Nietzsche was unlike Wagner's other followers. Though he was young, shy, and still fairly impressionable, he never completely turned all of his heart and mind over to Wagner. Unlike Karl Ritter, Otto Wesendonck, Hans von Bülow, and King Ludwig II, Nietzsche was unable to blind himself to the holes in Wagner's logic. In two years' time, the young philosopher, who had strong views of his own that he was not hesitant to put forth, would no longer accept every word Wagner uttered as truth. "I shuddered as I went on my way alone," he wrote, when he realized he must leave Wagner's powerful influence, "for I had never had anyone but Richard Wagner."

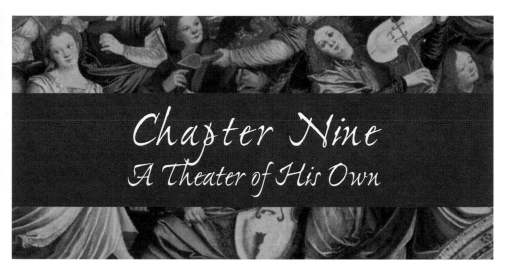

# Chapter Nine
## A Theater of His Own

After five months of silence, King Ludwig wrote to Wagner that he planned to continue giving him money for his living expenses despite all the trouble Wagner had caused him. Ludwig then informed him of plans to produce both *Tristan* and *Das Rheingold* in Munich. Wagner was against a full production of any of the *Ring* operas in Munich, because he felt the court theater did not have the resources to properly stage them. He wrote back suggesting that Munich do a concert performance instead—no sets or costumes, just the music. In the meantime, after a twelve-year lag, he resumed work on *Siegfried*.

Ludwig insisted on full productions; he owned the rights to the works and he could do with them as he wished. Wagner was still financially supported by the king, and so could not protest too much. But Bülow was no longer in

Munich, and Ludwig was not willing to use the new conductor, Karl Richter, who Wagner championed. Frustrated, Wagner left the Munich production alone, certain it would fail without his personal touch. He did not attend a single performance. *Rheingold* went over very well with the public, and Ludwig immediately ordered *Die Walküre* to be produced the following spring. He told Wagner to have *Siegfried* ready for a production in 1871.

In the summer of 1870, King Ludwig II ordered his army to join with the Prussians to mobilize against the French. The conflict was ostensibly over possession of territory that both Prussia and France claimed as theirs. However, Bismarck was determined to use the war against France as a way to unify Germany. He believed the war would stir up German nationalism and increase the drive toward the unification of the German states. In 1871, after the long, bitter siege of Paris, the war ended and Prussian king Karl Wilhelm I was pronounced *Kaiser* of the German Empire. Just as the war was beginning, Bülow went to Berlin, where he finally agreed to give Cosima a divorce. One month after the divorce was final, she and Wagner were married.

The following February, Wagner finished the full score of *Siegfried,* though he lied to the king about it to avoid having it staged right away. He then began working on the score for the final opera of the *Ring* cycle, *Götterdämmerung* or *The Twilight of the Gods.* Now that the cycle was close to completion, Wagner wanted more than ever to build a theater designed to present all four operas at one time. He knew the chances of getting this done in Munich were slim, so he and Cosima began to look for a suitable site. Richard Wagner, the man who had begun writing music without any instruction, conducted operas without training, and changed the form of opera without any guide, would find a way to have his theater built. He had no funding and no experience, but that had never stopped him before.

Cosima read in an encyclopedia that there was a theater in a town called Bayreuth that contained the largest stage ever built. They went to visit and found that, while the stage was indeed large, the opera house itself was not suited to the *Ring*. They were going to have to build a theater from scratch. Wagner went to Ludwig to ask for money, but the recent wars had drained his treasury and he worried his

This cartoon, which first appeared in the June 9, 1877 issue of *Illustrated Sporting and Dramatic News,* imagines how Wagner composed his difficult music.

subjects would be angry if he gave money to Wagner's project.

"If the theater at Bayreuth, built at the direction of Richard Wagner solely for the production of his works, and financed by private contributions, should become a reality . . . that fact alone may be counted one of the most remarkable events in the whole history of art and the greatest personal success of which any composer ever dreamed," wrote Eduard Hanslick when he heard of Wagner's plan. Never before had a theater been constructed to play only the works of one composer, and never had a composer built his own theater. Wagner planned a four-day festival for the theater he hoped would be built. The festival would feature a full performance of the *Ring* cycle—one opera each night. It would be unlike anything done before.

He set out on a massive campaign, speaking to members of the nobility and upper class all over Germany. He did concert tours and sold patron's certificates, which were like shares of stock, though there was no possibility for financial return. No tickets to the festival would be sold—anyone who donated would be invited as an honored guest. Some cities, including London and Chicago, offered greater support if he would change his location, but he

Influential music critic, Eduard Hanslick.
*(Courtesy of Bildarchiv der Oesterreichischen, Nationalbibliothek.)*

would not bend. The town of Bayreuth, hoping the theater would be good for their economy, had been supportive of his venture from the start. They also gave him a plot of land at no charge.

While he did fundraising, which would take the next three years, Wagner continued to work on the music for *The Twilight of the Gods*. He finished the score in July 1872, and the final orchestration in November 1874. Wagner was sixty-one years old. The *Ring* cycle had taken twenty-six years to complete.

Wagner's health began to slow him down. He confessed to Cosima that he was having heart trouble. Other observers had noticed that as Bayreuth plans fell further and further behind, Wagner often had "uncontrollable fits of rage," usually directed toward his wife, who was the one person always in his presence. One of Cosima's friends wrote, "On the whole it must be admitted that being the wife of a genius is not the easiest position in the world."

Despite his poor health, Wagner managed to accomplish what had seemed impossible. The Bayreuth theater was finally built. It took years of work, and when at last the theater was completed, it was unlike any place musicians and singers had ever before experienced. Wagner had made great innovations to the structure of an opera house. The critic Hanslick was once again impressed:

> The Wagner Theater itself is one of the most interesting and instructive of curiosities . . . because of the ingenious novelties of its interior arrangement.

The theater at Bayreuth.

Even the entrance to the auditorium is surprising: rows of seats rising in the style of an amphitheater in a semi-circle, behind them a low gallery, the Royal Box. Otherwise there are no boxes in the entire house. . . . Vision is equally good from every seat. One sees the proceedings on the stage without obstruction—and nothing else. At the beginning of a performance the auditorium is completely darkened; the brightly lighted stage . . . appears like a brilliantly colored picture in a dark frame.

Wagner's concept of a darkened auditorium was made possible because of the advent of electricity, as was the pit for the orchestra that Wagner had built underneath the stage. This innovation allowed the audience a clear view of the performers on stage, and also served to mute the orchestra enough that the singers' voices could be more clearly heard.

In the summer of 1875, rehearsals for the *Ring* began in earnest. It was a massive undertaking, involving sixteen hours of music, a huge cast, hundreds of sets, and an expanded orchestra. Karl Richter was hired to conduct, but Wagner directed all the acting and designed many of the backgrounds. There were problems, of course. The musicians were not used to being beneath the stage, and there was not enough space for 114 people and their instruments. Also, there was some trouble with the scenery: a mechanical dragon designed in Paris arrived in stages rather than all at once (the head was not present for the first performance, and the neck never made it at all). But in spite of the problems, a spirit of fun prevailed. Pranks abounded and merriment was to be had at the end of each long day. All in all, things were moving along successfully, and Wagner's concert tours continued to cover the expenses.

The Bayreuth Festival opened in the summer of 1876. The audience consisted of crowned heads from as far away as Brazil, musical icons like Liszt and the great Russian composer Peter Ilyich Tchaikovsky (composer of the *Nutcracker*), and all the wealthy patrons who had helped to create the theater. King Ludwig was there, marking the first time in eight years that Wagner and the king had been in each other's company. The only person noticeably absent was Hans von Bülow, who refused his invitation.

In the end, the performances were neither a triumph nor a complete disaster. The complicated leitmotif themes gave many theatergoers headaches. Each of the hundreds of leitmotifs conveyed a certain meaning: there was a sword

This painting depicts the opening scene of *Das Rheingold* as it was performed at Bayreuth, in which the Rhine Maidens appear to float while guarding their possession of gold. Painter Knut Ekwal published the above illustration in a Leipzig magazine, *Illustrirte Zeitung,* in 1876.

theme, a love theme, a tree theme, and so on. These themes often converged—when a sword pierces a tree, the tree theme is rudely interrupted by the sword motif. A Wagnerite, H. von Wolzogen, wrote a pamphlet titled "Thematic Guide" to help the frustrated listeners, and though no one wanted to admit to needing a copy, nearly every audience member had one.

While the music was a struggle, what everyone was talking about before and after the performances was food. Bayreuth was a provincial town and not prepared to handle so many visitors. There was hardly enough food to go around, nor was there any lodging to be spared. Hanslick wrote, "Not only are there no luxuries, often enough there are not even the necessities. I doubt that the enjoyment of art is furthered by being uncomfortably housed for a week, sleeping badly, eating wretchedly, and, after a strenuous five or six hours' performance of an opera, being uncertain of a modest snack." Ultimately, the festival was a financial disaster, and plunged Wagner deeper into debt. Repeating the festival the following summer was out of the question.

The Wagner family took a much-needed vacation to Italy that autumn, and there, Wagner and Nietzsche found themselves in each other's company for the last time. Nietzsche had been at the festival and was appalled by what he had seen there—fattened, wealthy patrons who seemed to care more for the parties than the music. Seeing Wagner courting them for their money disgusted him. The theater in Bayreuth was not a theater for the German people, Nietzsche complained; it was a theater for nobility. He saw no difference between

Friedrich Nietzsche.

Wagner's theater and any other court theater. Wagner was not the true German prophet, but an artist of excess and immorality he could no longer abide. From that point on, the two men never spoke again, and Nietzsche wrote highly critical essays about his former hero.

The debt Wagner acquired from building the Bayreuth theater left him no choice but to do more concerts. He spent the summer conducting in London, but his health was so poor he could not make it through an entire performance. The fees he received ended up being less than half of what he was originally offered. King Ludwig came to his aid once again, promising that any proceeds from Wagnerian operas played in Munich would go toward his debt. The condition of Ludwig's offer was that all of the *Ring* operas would have to be produced in Munich. Wagner did not want to see his *Ring* performed anywhere but Bayreuth, but he had no choice. He needed the money. The Munich productions opened a floodgate, and soon operas from the *Ring* were being played all over Europe. Wagner should have been elated, but he was bitter about the failure at Bayreuth. Even as royalties poured in, he continued to complain.

Now that his financial situation was stabilized and he was no longer touring, Wagner could begin work on his new opera, *Parsifal.* A retelling of one of Europe's most famous legends, it is the story of a young boy, Parsifal, who is destined to become a knight of the Holy Grail. The opera recounts the trials he goes through before attaining his goal.

Many critics, including Hanslick, thought it was strange that Wagner, who had written articles about how Christianity had ruined art, was writing an opera with an explicitly Christian theme. Some believed that as Wagner was nearing the end of his life he was becoming religious and atoning for former sins. Others argued that *Parsifal* was not about Wagner's love for Christianity, but about his hatred for the Jewish religion. After all, *Parsifal* denies that Christianity has its roots in Judaism. Once *Parsifal* was finished, Wagner wrote two articles that were published as appendixes to his opera, called "Religion and Art" and "Heroism and Christianity," which express his doubts that Jesus Christ was Jewish.

In May of 1882, preparations were underway for the second Bayreuth Festival, which was to include the premiere of *Parsifal.* Rehearsals were difficult because Wagner did not have the energy to direct his singers in his usual fashion. King Ludwig insisted that his new court conductor Hermann Levi conduct. Levi was Jewish. Wagner was appalled, but Ludwig gave him no choice. Levi put up with

A rendering of the colorful and dramatic set for Wagner's *Parsifal*.

name-calling and other verbal abuse from both Wagner and Cosima during the rehearsals, but such was his love for the music that he would not quit. Some of Levi's friends, including the composer Johannes Brahms, were angry with him for supporting Wagner's music, but Levi was steadfast. Though Wagner castigated him for his religion, the two actually got along, and Wagner would eventually ask Levi to conduct more of his work.

As with the *Ring,* Wagner wanted to have *Parsifal* performed only at the Bayreuth Festival. He was criticized for this since he claimed to be writing the music of the German people. If he was, his critics asked, how could the people of Germany hear it? Despite grumbling

German composer Johannes Brahms. His conservative Romantic style stood in great contrast to Wagner's own dramatic compositions. Controversy stewed between supporters of the two composers. *(Courtesy of the Library of Congress.)*

in the press about his attitudes and behavior, all sixteen of the performances sold out. At the final performance, unbeknownst to the audience, Wagner sneaked down into the orchestra pit and took the baton from Levi to conduct the last act himself. Perhaps he knew this would be his final musical act, and it was not just a farewell to Bayreuth, but to the world and to music. Levi wrote:

> At the end of the work the audience broke into applause that defies description. But the master did not show himself, but remained with us musicians, making bad jokes, and when the noise of the audience

showed no sign of abating after ten minutes, I shouted "Quiet! Quiet!" at the top of my voice. Then the master, still at the conductor's desk . . . spoke with such affection that everyone started to weep.

That September, Wagner left for Venice, Italy. He saw his friend Liszt before departing, and made plans with Levi for the next several festivals at Bayreuth. He wanted all of his operas, from *The Flying Dutchman* through *Parsifal,* performed there regularly. The only non-Wagner piece ever played at his theater would be Beethoven's *Ninth Symphony,* a work always near to his heart. As Wagner grew weaker, he spent most of his time at home.

On February 13, 1883, Wagner told his valet, "I shall have to take care of myself today," but he soon called out for a doctor. Cosima, according to her son Siegfried, heard him, and, rushing into his room, "ran into the half-open door so hard it almost split." She helped him to the couch, and, before the doctor could come, Richard Wagner died in her arms.

# Chapter Ten
## The Legacy

Richard Wagner's funeral was as lavish an affair as one would expect. A caravan of Venetian gondolas made its way to the train station with his coffin, and then, on the long, slow journey to Bayreuth, Cosima sat in a carriage alone beside her husband's remains. The Bayreuth station was crowded with mourners, and thousands of people lined the city streets to pay their respects. The following day, as snow fell, pallbearers placed the coffin into its grave at a site Wagner had chosen in the garden of his home. Cosima did not attend the funeral, and could not bear to go to his grave until half a century later, in 1930, when she would be laid beside him.

Richard Wagner's legacy is complicated. He wrote some of the most glorious, transcendent music of all time. He defined many theatrical conventions in use today, such as

Wagner is buried in the garden at Wahnfried, his house in Bayreuth.

the proscenium theater and the dimming of the house lights to completely immerse the audience in the drama. He also invented the curtain that opens from the center rather than being raised, and helped to establish a theatrical lighting design that is still in use. Though no composer would ever write in exactly the same style as Wagner, his work forever changed the way composers addressed their librettos.

Yet Wagner's musical innovations and genius must be taken in conjunction with what we know about his personality and his political beliefs. Years after Wagner's death, Cosima took a young painter and political agitator named Adolf Hitler under her wing. She provided him financial and emotional support and became his confidant. He became a devoted fan of Wagner's music and ideas. Later, as führer, or dictator, of Nazi Germany, Hitler came to Bayreuth every year to enjoy Wagner's operas. The Bayreuth Festival continued to be held during World War II. There, officials

Richard Wagner remains a controversial figure, musically and politically. *(Courtesy of Museo Teatro alla Scala, Milan.)*

of the Third Reich and honored soldiers were treated to performances of the nationalistic opera *Die Meistersinger* as guests of Hitler. Some of the battle strategies the Germans used during the war were named after characters in Wagner's librettos. One reason Hitler so admired Wagner was that they shared a deep anti-Semitism combined with a fervent belief in the glory and power of the German people. Many today still find it difficult to enjoy, or even to listen to, Wagner's music because his name is tainted by Hitler's adoration.

Wagner was not only an anti-Semite. He was also a liar, a philanderer, a cheat, and a manipulative schemer. Those people, including Minna, Cosima, Ludwig, and even Hermann Levi, who embraced him and his musical genius, loved him in spite of his faults. Some former fans of the artist, though, like Bülow and Nietzsche, eventually found his behavior and beliefs too odious to overlook.

Today Wagner's operas are performed around the world. The Bayreuth Festival continues and has a years-long waiting list for tickets. There are countless recordings of his operas, some legendary. Many of the performances have featured great Jewish artists, such as James Levine and Leonard Bernstein. Hundreds of books have been devoted to Wagner's life, his art, and his politics. The question, though, still remains: Is it possible to reconcile an appreciation for a great artist's work with an abhorrence for his personality and politics? It is a question each of us, as individuals, must answer for ourselves.

# Timeline

1813   On May 22, Richard Wagner is born in Leipzig, Germany; Friedrich Wagner dies in October; Richard's mother marries an actor named Ludwig Geyer and moves the family to Dresden.

1826   Composer Carl Maria von Weber dies; Wagner takes violin lessons, writes a play in the style of Shakespeare, and composes his first music.

1827   Composer Ludwig van Beethoven dies.

1830   Wagner meets opera diva Wilhelmine Schröder-Devrient; composes his Overture in B-flat.

1831   Wagner becomes a student at Leipzig University.

1832   Composes his Symphony in C Major and his first opera, *Die Hochzeit (The Wedding)*.

1833   In January, becomes choirmaster at Würzburg Theater; later, composes *Die Feen (The Fairies);* in the fall, composes *Das Liebesverbot* (*The Love Ban*) and becomes conductor of the Magdeburg Theater Company; falls in love with actress Minna Planer.

1836   *Das Liebesverbot* is performed for the only time while Wagner is living; on November 24, Wagner marries Minna Planer.

1837   Begins composing *Rienzi;* in August, Wagner takes post as director of Riga Theater.

1839   Wagner moves to Paris.

1840   Begins writing articles for *Gazette Musicale;* composes
       one-act version of *Der Fliegande Holländer (The Flying
       Dutchman)* for the Paris Grand Opera.

1841   Completes three-act version of *The Flying Dutchman.*

1842   *Rienzi* and *The Flying Dutchman* are scheduled for
       performance in Dresden.

1843   Wagner takes post as kapellmeister at Dresden Court.

1845   Wagner meets composer Franz Liszt at Berlin premiere
       of *The Flying Dutchman;* completes *Tannhäuser.*

1848   Wagner's mother dies; Wagner completes *Lohengrin;*
       in June, Wagner is swept up in revolutionary spirit after
       the French overthrow King Louis Philippe.

1849   Exiled from Germany, he moves to Zürich, Switzerland.

1850   Wagner meets young apprentices Karl Ritter and Hans
       von Bülow.

1851   Writes treatise *Opera and Drama;* meets Mathilda and
       Otto Wesendonck.

1852   Writes article "Judaism in Music"; writes librettos for
       *Der Ring des Nibelungen.*

1854   Completes scores to *Das Rhinegold* and *Die Walküre.*

1857   Otto Wesendonck loans his house in Switzerland to
       Wagner; Wagner begins composing *Tristan and Isolde*
       for Mathilde Wesendonck; meets Bülow's new
       wife, Cosima.

1861   Wagner is allowed to return to Vienna.

1863   Begins composing *Die Meistersinger;* is given permis-
       sion to re-enter Saxony; asks Minna for a divorce, which
       she refuses; sees Minna for the last time.

1864   November, Wagner and Cosima von Bülow begin their
       love affair.

1865   King Ludwig II of Bavaria becomes Wagner's patron;
       Ludwig Schnorr, the star of *Tristan and Isolde* dies,
       reigniting a myth that the opera is cursed; Wagner

begins writing his autobiography *Mien Leiben.*

1866 War between Austria and Prussia breaks out.

1868 On June 21, *Die Meistersinger* premieres in Munich.

1869 Cosima moves in with Wagner; Wagner meets the philosopher Friedrich Nietzche.

1870 On July 18, Bülow divorces Cosima; one month later, she marries Wagner.

1871 In February, Wagner completes score to *Siegfried.*

1872 In July, Wagner completes the final opera of the *Ring* cycle, a twenty-six-year effort.

1876 The first Bayreuth Festival is held, featuring the performance of the entire *Ring* cycle.

1882 Wagner's *Parsifal* is performed at Bayreuth.

1883 On February 13, Wagner dies in Cosima's arms.

# Glossary of Musical Terms

**amphitheater** A circular auditorium with seats arranged in rising tiers around a central stage.

**aria** A solo in an opera used to demonstrate both the emotion of the character and the vocal abilities of the singer.

**ballet** A classical form of dance, incorporating movement, music, and scenery to convey a story, theme, or atmosphere.

**Baroque era** A period in history that dates roughly from 1600 to 1750. The most famous composers from this era are Bach, Vivaldi, and Handel.

**benefactor** Someone who funds an artist.

**brass band** A music ensemble consisting of horns and drums.

**choirmaster** A person who teaches and leads a chorus of singers.

**chorus** An ensemble of singers.

**Classical period** A period in history that dates roughly from 1750 to 1830. The most famous composers from this era are Mozart, Haydn, and Beethoven.

**composer** One who writes music.

**concert** A performance of music.

**conductor** The director of a musical ensemble.

**counterpoint** Two or more melodies written to be performed simultaneously.

**court theater** A performance space under the control of the reigning king or duke.

**critic** A person who writes reviews of performances.

**dialogue** Conversation between the characters of an opera or play.

**epic** A long story or poem, usually concerning a historical legend.

**fugue** A musical form in which an intial melody is changed, rearranged, and repeated many times to produce a complicated, tapestry-like texture.

**kapellmeister** The musical director and conductor of a court emsemble.

**leitmotifs** Thematic musical elements in an opera or symphony that represent specific characters, ideas, or emotions.

**libretto** Italian for *little book;* the text of an opera.

**lieder** A German word meaning songs written for piano and voice.

**melody** The main tune of a song or instrumental piece.

**modulate** To raise or lower the notes of the music from one key to another.

**monologue** When a character in an opera or play sings or speaks alone.

**movement** The division of large pieces of music into independent sections. Each movement in a compositon is usually defined by a particular speed or character.

**music publisher** A person or company that prints music scores and sells the copies.

**musical director** A person who directs the orchestra and singers in a production.

**musicians** People who sing or play instruments. In Wagner's day, directors and conductors were considered musicians as well.

**one-act** A play or opera that has no intermission.

**opera** Originating in seventeenth-century Italy, a story set to music, usually entirely sung. Music, drama, scenery, costumes, dance, and other theatrical elements combine to make the art form complete. In nineteenth-century France, a style of opera known as grand opera was developed, which incorporated elaborate ballets and huge choruses. Comedic operas are called by the Italian term *opera buffa,* or in French, *opera comique.*

**oratorio** Usually Biblical stories set to music. As with opera, these stories are sung, but (unlike opera) oratorios do not make use of elaborate staging.

**orchestra** A group of instruments divided into wind, brass, percussion, and string sections.

**orchestration** The act of determining which instrument will play which section of a musical score.

**overture** The music at the beginning of an opera, musical, or play, though often overtures are played in concert as separate works.

**piano** An instrument with eighty-eight keys. Hammers, corresponding to the keys, strike strings to produce the piano's sound. A grand piano is a larger piano in a horizontal harp-shaped frame usually supported on three legs.

**Philharmonic** A symphony orchestra.

**premiere** The first performance of a new piece of music.

**production** When an opera or play is staged for performance.

**program** A printed guide for audience members at a concert, play, or opera performance that explains the music or story to be presented.

**recitatives** The conversation sections used to further the plot in an opera.

**rehearsal** A session in which actors, singers and instrumentalists practice for a performance.

**repertoire** The list of pieces that a given performer or ensemble is prepared to perform.

**Romantic era** A period in history that dates roughly from 1830 to 1900. Some of the most famous composers from this era are Brahms, Mendelssohn, and Wagner.

**royalties** The fees collected by the artist for the sale or performance of his or her work.

**saga** A long story.

**score** A musical composition in written form.

**soloist** An individual who sings or plays an instrument alone.

**sonata** A composition for a solo or accompanied instrument, usually in three or four movements of varying tempo.

**soprano** The highest female voice in a choir.

**stage manager** An assistant to the director, the stage manager works offstage supervising the production as it takes place onstage.

**string quartet** A piece of music scored for two violins, viola, and cello. Also, the group of four musicians which performs this music.

**symphony** A large-scale instrumental work, scored for full orchestra, in four movements.

**tenor** The highest natural male voice in a choir.

**theater director** The person who controls the business dealings of a theater and chooses the plays or operas that will be produced.

**theater manager** The person who controls the activities of a theatrical production, including budgets, casting, and organizing rehearsals.

**theatrical troupe** A group of actors, singers, and instrumentalists that perform plays and operas.

**timpani** A set of one or more kettledrums, used in orchestras.

**tour** When a musician or theatrical troupe travels from city to city staging performances.

**violin** A four-stringed musical instrument played with a bow.

**virtuoso** An expert performer on a particular instrument.

# Sources

**CHAPTER ONE: Growing Up in the Theater**

p. 11, "and said that we loved each other . . ." Derek Watson, *Richard Wagner: A Biography* (New York: Schirmer, 1979), 267.

p. 26, "if in the days to come she should ever hear . . ." Richard Wagner, *My Life* (New York: Da Capo Press, 1992), 44.

**CHAPTER TWO: Conducting and Composing**

p. 30, "independence" Wagner, *My Life,* 68.

p. 37, "inconceivable charm" Ibid., 99.

p. 39, "My association with my kindly . . ." Ibid., 89.

p. 40, "bigwigs of opera" Ibid., 114.

p. 45, "Not a little embarrassed . . ." Ibid., 163.

**CHAPTER THREE: Paris**

p. 51, "hack-work" Wagner, *My Life,* 256.

p. 57, "At last, the hour . . ." Ibid., 216.

**CHAPTER FOUR: Success and Revolution**

p. 60, "No subsequent experience . . ." Wagner, *My Life,* 231.

p. 65, "If there is anyone . . ." Eduard Hanslick, *Vienna's Golden Years of Music, 1850-1900* (New York: Simon and Schuster, 1950), 23.

p. 69, "the downfall of the last glimmer . . ." Hans Mayer, *Portrait of Wagner* (New York: Herder and Herder, 1972), 63.

p. 70, "dull agitation" Wagner, *My Life,* 472.

**CHAPTER FIVE: From Exile to the *Ring***
p. 73, "What sort of future do I face?" Watson, *Richard Wagner,* 109.
p. 74, "not only did I hate the idea . . ." Wagner, *My Life,* 523.
p. 74, "felt . . . weak and broke out in . . ." Ibid., 525.
p. 75, "Deliverance from this hell is all I wish for." Watson, *Richard Wagner,* 112.
p. 76, "marking the various times at which the performance presumably began . . ." Wagner, *My Life,* 547.
p. 77, "The general enthusiasm would in any case . . ." Hanslick, *Vienna's Golden Years of Music,* 51.
p. 83, "I still felt the peculiar disinclination and fear . . ." Wagner, *My Life,* 600.
p. 83, "I suddenly had the feeling . . ." Ibid., 499.

**CHAPTER SIX: The Muse and the Music**
p. 85, "the society began . . .to regret . . ." Wagner, *My Life,* 624.
p. 89, "I remember that I never once looked back . . ." Ibid., 689.

**CHAPTER SEVEN: Homeless in the Homeland**
p. 92, "base of operations" Wagner, *My Life,* 652.
p. 94, "my *Meistersinger* poem swelled daily . . ." Ibid., 673.
p. 95, "Good Gracious!... such sums as I might *earn* . . ." Alice Hunt Sokoloff, *Cosima Wagner, Extraordinary Daughter of Franz Liszt* (New York: Dodd, Mead & Co., 1969), 118-9.
p. 96, "In time our jesting died away in silence . . ." Wagner, *My Life,* 729.
p. 96, "Only a miracle can save me now." Watson, *Richard Wagner,* 194.
p. 97, "It would on the other hand . . ." Mayer, *Portrait of Wagner,* 114.

**CHAPTER EIGHT: The King**
p. 100, "venerate [Wagner] like a God" Bryan Magee, *Aspects of Wagner* (New York: Stein and Day Publishers, 1969), 59.

p. 103, "received sufficient support from my absent . . ." Watson, *Richard Wagner,* 232.

p. 104, "So long as I am King I cannot be united . . ." Ernest Newman, *The Life of Richard Wagner, volume 4* (New York: Alfred A. Knopf, 1946), 4-5.

p. 106, "Since February of 1865 . . ." Sokoloff, *Cosima Wagner,* 181.

p. 107, "a further post with a fixed salary" Newman, *The Life of Richard Wagner,* 62.

p. 109, "truly cracked." William Berger, *Wagner Without Fear* (New York: Vintage Books, 1998), 40.

p. 109, "all men are brothers whatever their religion." Ibid., 40.

p. 110, "I shuddered as I went on my way alone . . ." Sokoloff, *Cosima Wagner,* 232.

**CHAPTER NINE: A Theater of His Own**

p. 114, "If the theater at Bayreuth, built at the direction of Richard Wagner..." Hanslick, *Vienna's Golden Years of Music,* 139.

p. 115, "uncontrollable fits of rage" Sokoloff, *Cosima Wagner,* 247.

p. 115, "On the whole it must be admitted that being the wife of a genius . . ." Ibid., 247-8.

p. 115, "The Wagner Theater itself is one of the most interesting and instructive of curiosities . . ." Hanslick, *Vienna's Golden Years of Music,* 151.

p. 119, "Not only are there no luxuries," Ibid., 148-9.

p. 123, "At the end of the work the audience broke into applause that . . ." Watson, *Richard Wagner,* 312.

p. 124, "I shall have to take care of myself today," Ibid., 314.

p. 124, "...ran into the half-open door so hard it almost split." Ibid., 314.

# Bibliography

Bergamini, Andrea. *Beethoven and the Classical Age*. Hauppauge, NY: Barron's Educational Series, Inc., 1999.

Berger, William. *Wagner Without Fear*. New York: Vintage Books, 1998.

Cavalletti, Carlo. *Chopin and the Romantic Age*. Hauppauge, NY: Barron's Educational Series, Inc., 2000.

Hanslick, Eduard. *Vienna's Golden Years of Music, 1850-1900*. New York: Simon and Schuster, 1950.

Magee, Bryan. *Aspects of Wagner*. New York: Stein and Day Publishers, 1969.

Mayer, Hans. *Portrait of Wagner*. New York: Herder and Herder, 1972.

McSpadden, J. Walker. *Operas and Musical Comedies*. New York: Thomas Y. Crowell Company, 1951.

Millington, Barry. *Wagner*. New Jersey: Princeton University Press, 1992.

Newman, Ernest. *The Life of Richard Wagner*, volumes 1-4. New York: Alfred A. Knopf, 1946.

Osborne, Charles. *Wagner and His World*. New York: Charles Scribner's Sons, 1977.

Padmore, Elaine. *The Great Composers: Wagner*. New York: Thomas Y. Crowell Company, 1971.

2

Sokoloff, Alice Hunt. *Cosima Wagner, Extraordinary Daughter of Franz Liszt*. New York: Dodd, Mead & Company, 1969.

Wagner, Richard. *The Art-Work of the Future and Other Works*. Lincoln: University of Nebraska Press, 1993.

———. *My Life*. New York: Da Capo Press, 1992.

Watson, Derek. *Richard Wagner: A Biography*. New York: Schirmer, 1979.

# Web sites

**Harvard Biographical Dictionary of Music**
**www.hup.harvard.edu/features/ranhab**
Edited by Don Michael Randel, featuring a complete, detailed
entry on Richard Wagner.

**Humanities Web**
**www.humanitiesweb.org**
A well-organized source of information on music from the
Medieval period through the present. Also covers literature,
visual arts, and history.

**The Internet Public Library's Music History 102**
**www.ipl.org/div/mushist**
A guide to Western composers and their music from the Middle
Ages to the present.

**Richard Wagner Museum**
**www.wagnermuseum.de/**

**Wonderful World of Music History**
**www.chsdragonband.com**
Offers a general overview of periods in music history, biographical information on composers, and links to other helpful
sites. Maintained by high-school music students.

# Index